BOOKS BY MAX BEERBOHM

Collected Essays, Criticism, Short Stories, Etc.

The Works of Max Beerbohm
More
Yet Again
And Even Now
A Variety of Things
Mainly on the Air
Around Theatres

Stories, Character Sketches

The Happy Hypocrite
A Christmas Garland (Parodies)
Seven Men (*reissued in* 1950 *as* Seven Men and Two
  Others)
The Dreadful Dragon of Hay Hill

Novel

Zuleika Dobson

Caricatures, Cartoons

Caricatures of Twenty-five Gentlemen
The Poet's Corner
A Book of Caricatures
The Second Childhood of John Bull
Fifty Caricatures
A Survey
Rossetti and His Circle
Things New and Old
Observations

Mainly on the Air

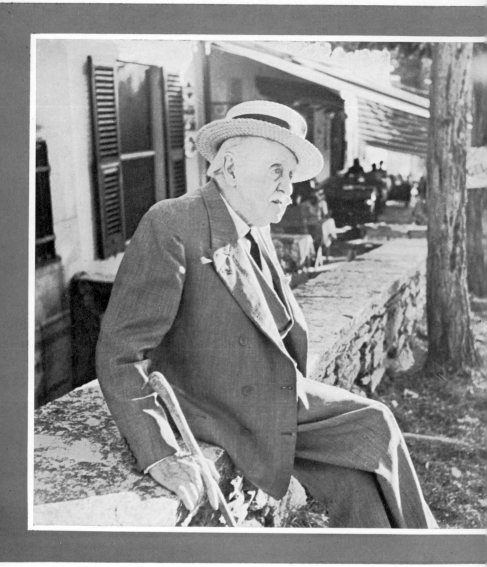

Max Beerbohm *a portrait by Cecil Beaton*

MAINLY

ON THE AIR

Max Beerbohm

NEW YORK

Alfred·A·Knopf

1958

L. C. Catalog card number: 58–9967
© *Elizabeth Beerbohm, 1957*

THIS IS A BORZOI BOOK,
PUBLISHED BY ALFRED A. KNOPF, INC.

FIRST AMERICAN EDITION

Author's Note

I FEAR that an apology should be made to any reader of the six broadcasts that form the first part of this book. They were composed for the ears of listeners; and though of course a writer should always write not less for the ear than for the eye of the reader, he does not, in writing for the ear only, express himself in just the way that would be his if he were writing for the eye as well. He trusts the inflexions of his voice to carry the finer shades of his meaning and of his feeling. He does not take his customary pains to make mere typography leave no barrier between his reader and him. I would therefore take the liberty of advising you to read these broadcasts aloud to yourself— or to ask some friend to read them aloud to you.

I have included in the book six other things—narrowcasts, as it were. The first of these appeared in *The Windmill*, the second and fourth in *World Review*, the third in *The Carthusian*, the fifth in *The Cornhill*, and the sixth in *The London Mercury* (and afterwards in one of the volumes of a limited edition of my writings).

The broadcasts all appeared in *The Listener*; and some portions of "Speed" were, I am pleased to say, used by the Pedestrians' Association as a pamphlet.

[1946]   M.B.

PUBLISHER'S NOTE

   The new, enlarged edition contains eight additional essays and talks broadcast on the B.B.C., London; they appeared, with the exception of "Marie Lloyd" and "An Incident," in *The Listener*. "Lytton Strachey," the Cambridge University Rede Lecture for 1943, was published as a small book in 1943. In the first section, the date of broadcast is given below the title; the date of composition, in the case of pieces not originally written for broadcasting, is given at the end.

CONTENTS

BROADCASTS

CONTENTS

OTHER THINGS

Broadcasts

LONDON REVISITED

[Sunday, 29 December 1935]

ONE OF THE GREATEST OF ENGLISHMEN said that the man who is tired of London is tired of life.

Well, Dr. Johnson had a way of being right. But he had a way of being wrong too—otherwise we shouldn't love him so much. And I think that a man who is tired of London may merely be tired of life *in London*. He won't, certainly, feel any such fatigue if he was born and bred in a distant county, and came to London and beheld London only when he had reached maturity. Almost all the impassioned lovers of London have spent, like Dr. Johnson, their childhood and adolescence in the country. Such was not my own fate. I was born within sound of Bow Bells. I am, in fact, a genuine Cockney (as you will already have guessed from my accent). Before I was able to speak or think, my eyes must have been familiar with endless vistas of streets; countless people passing by without a glance at the dear little fellow in the perambulator; any number of cart-horses drawing carts, cab-horses drawing cabs, carriage-horses drawing carriages, through the more or less smoke-laden atmosphere. I was smoke-dried before I could reason and prattle. For me there was never the great apocalyptic moment of initiation into the fabulous metropolis. I never said, "So this—is London!"

Years passed: I became a small boy. And I daresay I used to exclaim, "So these are Kensington Gardens!" I liked the grass and the trees. But there were the railings that bounded them, and the pavements and thoroughfares beyond the railings. These had no magic for me. It was the country—the *real* country—the not imitation country—that I loved.

I became a young man. London was the obvious place for me to earn a living in. In my native city I abode until the year 1910, at which time I was thirty-seven years old. Then I escaped. I had known some parts of the vast affair pretty well. I wish I had appreciated their beauty more vividly while it lasted: a beauty that is gone—or all but gone. I am going to be depressing. Perhaps you had better switch me off.

London is a Cathedral town. And in my day—in the 'eighties of my boyhood and the 'nineties of my youth—London, with all her faults, seemed not wholly unlike a Cathedral town, I do assure you. There was a demure poetry about her: one could think of her as "her": nowadays she cannot be called "she": she is essentially "it." Down by the docks, along the Mile End Road, throughout the arid reaches of South Kensington, and so on, I daresay she was "it" already; full of later-nineteenth-century utilitarianism and efficiency, throwing out harsh hints of what the twentieth century had up its horrid sleeve. But in such districts as I liked and, whenever I could, frequented, she kept the eighteenth century about her. Hampstead, upon its hill, was a little old remote village; and so was Chelsea, down yonder by the river. Mayfair and Westminster and St. James's were grand, of course, very urban, in a proudly unostentatious way. There were Victorian intrusions here and there in their architecture. But the eighteenth century still beautifully reigned over them. They were places of leisure—of *leesure,* one might almost have said in the old-fashioned way. And, very urban though they were, they were not incongruous with rusticity. St. James's Park seemed a natural appanage to St. James's Street; and the two milkmaids who milked two cows there, and sold the milk, did not seem strangely romantic. The Green Park seemed not out of keeping with the houses of Piccadilly. Nor did the Piccadilly goat strike one as more than a little odd in Piccadilly.

I don't know much about him, though I so often saw him and liked him so much. He lived in a large mews in a side-street, opposite to Gloucester House, the home of the venerable Duke of Cambridge. At about ten o'clock in the morning he would come treading forth with a delicately clumsy gait down the side-street—come very slowly, as though not quite sure there mightn't be some grass for him to nibble at between the paving-stones. Then he would pause at the corner of Piccadilly and flop down against the railings of the nearest house. He would remain there till luncheon-time and return in the early afternoon. He was a large, handsome creature, with great intelligence in his amber eyes. He never slept. He was always interested in the passing scene. I think nothing escaped him. I wish he could have written his memoirs when he finally retired. He had seen, day by day, much that was worth seeing.

He had seen a constant procession of the best-built vehicles in the world, drawn by very beautifully bred and beautifully groomed and beautifully harnessed horses, and containing very ornate people. Vehicles of the most diverse kinds. High-swung barouches, with immense armorial bearings on their panels, driven by fat, white-wigged coachmen, and having powdered footmen up behind them; signorial phaetons; daring tandems; discreet little broughams, brown or yellow; flippant high dog-carts; low but flippant Ralli-carts; very frivolous private hansoms shaming the more serious public ones. And all these vehicles went by with a cheerful briskness; there was hardly ever a block for them in the traffic. And their occupants were very visible and were looking their best. The occupants of those low-roofed machines which are so pitifully blocked nowadays all along Piccadilly may, for aught one knows, be looking their best. But they aren't on view. The student of humanity must be content to observe the pedestrians.

These, I fear, would pain my old friend the goat. He was accustomed to what was called the man-about-town —a now extinct species, a lost relic of the eighteenth century and of the days before the great Reform Bill of 1831; a leisurely personage, attired with great elaboration, on his way to one of his many clubs; not necessarily interesting in himself; but fraught with external character and point: very satisfactory to those for whom the visible world exists. From a sociological standpoint perhaps he was all wrong, and perhaps his successor—the earnest fellow in a "trilby" and a "burberry" and a pair of horn-rimmed spectacles, hurrying along to his job—or in quest of some job—is all right. But one does rather wish the successor looked as if he felt himself to be all right. Let him look serious by all means. But need he look so nervous? He needs must. He doesn't want to be killed, he doesn't even want to be maimed, at the next crossing. He must keep his wits about him. I advise him to dash down with me into one of the Tubes. He will be safer there, as were the early Christians in the catacombs.

They are not beautiful, these Tubes; nor are they even interesting in character, except to engineers. But are the streets above them beautiful—or interesting in character —nowadays, to anybody of my own kind and age? London never had any formal or obvious beauty, such as you find in Paris; or any great, overwhelming grandeur, such as Rome has. But the districts for which I loved her, and several other districts too, had a queer beauty of their own, and were intensely characteristic—inalienably Londonish. To an intelligent foreigner, visiting London for the first time, what would you hasten to show? Except some remnants here and there, and some devious little nooks, there is nothing that would excite or impress him. The general effect of the buildings that have sprung up everywhere in recent years is not such an effect as the intelligent foreigner may not have seen in divers other places—Chicago, for example, or Berlin, or Pittsburgh. London has been cosmopolitanised, democratised, commercialised, mechanised, standardised, vulgarised, so extensively that one's pride in showing it to a foreigner is changed to a wholesome humility. One feels rather as Virgil may have felt in showing Hell to Dante.

It is a bright, cheerful, salubrious Hell, certainly. But still—to *my* mind—Hell. In some ways a better place, I readily concede, than it was in my day, and in days before mine. Heinrich Heine was horrified by the poverty—the squalor and starvation—that abounded in the midst of the immense wealth and splendour. Some years later Gavarni's soul was shocked by it; and then Dostoievsky's; and presently Monsieur Ludovic Halévy's; and in due course Mr. Henry James's. I too am human. I am therefore glad that Seven Dials—and similar places which I used to skirt with romantic horror—are gone. Had I been acting as guide to those distinguished visitors, I should have tried to convince them that no such places existed, save in the creative alien fancy. But I ask myself: Suppose those illustrious visitors rose from their graves today and asked me to show them round the sights that would best please their aesthetic sensibilities in the London of this year of grace, what should I say, what do, in my patriotic embarrassment? I suppose I would, with vague waves of the hand, stammeringly redirect them to their graves.

I could not ask them to accompany me along Piccadilly or up Park Lane, to admire the vast excesses of contemporary architecture. I could not say to them, "Never mind the rasure of certain unassuming houses that were called 'great houses' in your day—and in mine. Cast up your eyes—up, up, up!—at the houses that have displaced them. Try to count the little uniform slits that serve as windows in the splendid ferro-concrete surface. Admire the austerity of the infinite *ensemble*. Think how inspiring to the historic imagination it will all be, a century or so hence!" I couldn't speak thus, for I cannot imagine any history being made in these appallingly bleak yet garish tenements. Or, at any rate, I refuse to suppose that they or any of the similar monstrosities that have been springing up in all the more eligible districts could ever take on an historic tone. They will continue to look like—what shall I say?—what *do* they look like?—improper workhouses.

Odious though they are in themselves, one might not hate them much if one found them on some barren plain in (say) the middle-west of America—some plain as barren and as meaningless as they. But when one thinks of the significant houses, the old habitable homes, that were demolished to make way for them, and when one sees how what remains of decent human architecture is reduced by them to the scale of hardly noticeable hovels, then one's heart sickens, and one's tongue curses the age into which one has survived. A few years ago, in the Print Room of the British Museum, Mr. Laurence Binyon showed me a very ancient little water-colour drawing. The foreground of it was a rather steep grassy slope. At the foot of the slope stood a single building, which I at once recognised as St. James's Palace. Beyond the Palace were stretches of green meadows; and far away there was just one building —the Abbey of Westminster. And I thought how pained the artist would have been if he had foreseen the coming of St. James's Street. I felt sure that he, like myself, preferred the country to any town. Yet I could not find it in my heart to deplore the making of that steep little street, destined to be so full of character and history. I could only regret that my favourite street was being steadily degraded, year after year, by the constructive vandals. There are no actual skyscrapers in it, as yet. But already the Palace cuts a poor figure. And the lovely façade of Boodle's is sadly squat. And a certain little old but ever young shop that stands somewhere between those two is hardly visible to the naked eye. I would affectionately name it, were I not so anxious to obey the B.B.C.'s admirable ban on that greatest of all modern pests, the advertiser.

Regent Street, Nash's masterpiece, which is mourned so bitterly by so many people, was never very dear to my heart, even before the days when Norman Shaw's pseudo-Florentine fortress suddenly sprang up and ruined the scale of its quadrant and all the rest of it. Its tone was always rather vulgar. It was never anything but a happy hunting-ground for ardent shoppers. Nothing but shopping had ever happened in it. But it was a noble design. And when its wide road and pavements were empty in the dawn, and its level copings were pale against the smokeless sky, the great long strong curve of the smooth-faced houses had a beauty that I shall not forget. I conceive that the pretentious chaos now reigning in its stead must in the quiet magic of the dawn be especially nasty.

It was the Squares, that particular glory of London, that I loved best of all. Their green centres have not yet been built over, for some reason. I look with pleasure at their surviving grass and trees. But I try not to see from the corners of my eyes what has happened to their architecture. St. James's Square, the finest of them all, has been wrecked utterly. Berkeley Square, which was a good second, has suffered a like fate. So has Portman Square. Dear little Kensington Square has been saved, by the obstinacy of some enlightened tenants, from the clutches of Mammon. Bedford Square is intact, as yet. Let us be thankful, before it is too late, for much of Bloomsbury.

The London University is about to play the deuce there. I suppose the Inns of Court, those four sanctuaries of civilisation, are safe in the adroit hands of the lawyers. Parliament will not be able to betray *them,* as she has betrayed that other sanctuary, the Adelphi.

I revisit England and London at intervals of two or three years; and every time I find that the havoc that has been wrought in my absence is more than ever extensive. How do I contrive to bear it? Let me reveal that secret. As I go my rounds, I imagine that the present is the past. I imagine myself a man of the twenty-first century, a person with an historic sense, whose prayer that he should behold the London of a hundred years ago has been granted. And my heart is thrilled with rapture. Look! There's a horse drawing a cart! And look! There's a quite small house—a lovely little thing that looks as though it had been built by the hand of man, and as though a man might quite pleasantly live in it. It has a chimney, with smoke coming out of it. And there's a coal-heaver. And there's—it must be—it *is*—a muffin-man!

By such devices of make-believe do I somewhat console and brace myself. But there is always a deadweight of sadness in me. Selfish sadness: I ought to keep my pity for the young people who never saw what I have seen, who will live to see what I shall not see—future great vistas of more and more commercialism, more machinery, more standardisation, more nullity.

I warned you that I was going to be depressing. I wish I hadn't kept my word. I might well have broken it on an evening so soon after Christmas, so soon before the New Year. Forget this talk. Or at any rate discount it. Remember that after all I'm an old fogey—and perhaps rather an old fool. And let me assure you that I'm cheerful company enough whenever I'm not in London and not thinking of London. And now I'm just off to the country. I have arranged to be driven straight from Broadcasting House to Paddington. I shall *just* catch the train.—I wish you all a very happy New Year—somewhere in the country.—I hope I haven't advertised Paddington.—Ladies and Gentlemen, goodnight.

SPEED

[Sunday, 26 April 1936]

In the Eye of the Lord,
By the Will of the Lord,
Out of the infinite
Bounty dissembled,
Since Time began,
In the Hand of the Lord,
Speed!

Speed as a chattel:
Speed in your daily
Account and economy;
One with your wines,
And your books and your bath—

Speed!
Speed as a rapture:
An integral element
In the new scheme of Life
Which the good Lord, the Master,
Wills well you should frame
In the light of His laugh
And His great, His ungrudging,
His reasoned benevolence—
Speed!

THESE WORDS, Ladies and Gentlemen, are not mine. They are the words of a man far more remarkable than I: William Ernest Henley, poet and critic, editor of *The Scots Observer*, a great inspirer of youth. The light of his fame is dim now; but it shone fiercely in the eighteen-nineties, and after. He himself was a fierce fellow enough. He had the head of a Viking, and the torso of a Viking; but from his early manhood he had been crippled by ill-health, insomuch that he could walk only with the help of crutches—he, who should have gone ever swinging over hill and dale, to satiate his vitality. In the very early years of this century, in the very early days of motoring, young Mr. Alfred Harmsworth, who was one of his great admirers, took him out for a long drive into the country. At last Henley went swinging over hill and dale. The Mercédes was for him a glorious revelation, an apocalypse. His Muse vibrantly responded, and he wrote the fine poem of which I have read to you the opening lines.

In those days even a quite prosaic and quite agile person, seated in a motor-car, felt something of that fine frenzy which filled Henley's breast. Cars were not the things they are now. You didn't have to creep into them and crouch *in* them and squirm *out* of them. They were wide-open to the elements, and wind-screens were unknown. And in fine dry weather, as you sped along the roads at what seemed then a terrific pace, the air rushed into your lungs with the utmost violence, making a new man of you—and a better man of you. So as not to be blinded with dust, you wore large goggles over your eyes. But dust entered into your ears and nostrils and into the very pores of your skin. And all the while you were moving not forward merely. The machine was such that you were continuously bobbing up and down, and oscillating from side to side. Your body was taking an immense amount of wholesome exercise. Insomuch that when the ride was over, and you had gone and vigorously shampooed the dust away from you, you felt that you were now an even newer and a still better man.

I, at any rate, used to have that conviction about myself. And if I had been a poet—and a generaliser, as every poet is—I should doubtless have tried to found on my experience some great philosophic moral. Henley was not content to have had a joy-ride. The joy of his ride had to be brought into close relation to the cosmos. It must be shown that the life of mankind on this planet had been immensely and for ever enriched by the internal combustion engine. Said Henley:

> The heart of Man
> Tears at Man's destiny
> Ever; and ever

> Makes what it may
> Of his wretched occasions,
> His infinitesimal
> Portion in Time.

Hence the Mercédes!

And by the discovery of the Mercédes our portion in Time was to be very appreciably and very agreeably magnified.

Henley had not any religion of an ecclesiastical kind. But he was nevertheless a deeply religious man. He had made a god of Literature. He had made a god of the British Empire. He had made a god also of the Tory Party. And here was a new god for him—Speed. If someone had asked him whether the invention of the steam-engine and the railroad had greatly blessed our lot, he might have looked rather dubious. For he was, despite his Imperialism, essentially an eighteenth-century man, and Victorian things did not arride him. But his faith in the universal beneficence of the Mercédes showed that he was, after all, in one respect, rather belatedly, a true Victorian. He believed, as we, alas!—we distressful moderns—no longer do, in the idea of Progress. I rather doubt whether, if he were living today, in a world that has succumbed so meekly to the ideal of speed—speed everywhere and at all times, produced by means of machinery and regarded as an end in itself—he would maintain that we had added a cubit to our stature.

In a sense, mankind has always loved speed. Speed here and there, speed in season, has always been acknowledged to be great fun. The Marathon race was a very popular institution. So were the Roman chariot races. One is probably right in supposing that Adam and Eve used often to race each other round the Garden of Eden, very blithely. Dick Turpin's exploit on Black Bess would have commended itself in any era to the people of any nation. So would even the involuntary adventure of John Gilpin. Dear to us all is the thought of Puck putting a girdle round the earth in forty minutes. Long live the Derby, and the Grand National! All honour to young Mr. Timpson, of Trinity College, Cambridge, who walked, the other day, to St. Paul's Cathedral and back in twenty-three hours, for a wager. Even that occasional squadron of stockbrokers marching from London to an hotel in Brighton rather thrills the heart . . . or doesn't it? Charles Dickens never wrote anything more exhilarating than the Pickwickians' journey by coach to Rochester. De Quincey was at his very best on the subject of the Eclipse coach. Coaches seem, indeed, to have been a godsend to all novelists and essayists. There was magic in them, evidently. They are not romantic to us alone: they were so to their contemporaries. Railway-trains were romantic for a few years. In the memoirs or diaries of the Victorians you will find that the first journey by rail made as deep a dint on sensibility as did the Duke of Wellington's funeral, or the first visit to the Crystal Palace. Well might those early passengers have prayed,

> Lord, send a man like Bobbie Burns
> To sing the Song of Steam!

But many years were to elapse before Mr. Kipling came, combining with an immense gift for verse a mystical adoration of machinery. "Romance brought up the nine-fifteen," said Mr. Kipling. But, we ask ourselves, did it? Wasn't it rather the engine-man and the stoker? And we ask ourselves whether they perhaps are romantic figures, and we hope that we can answer in the affirmative; but— well, it would seem that in machinery there is for most of us something non-conductive of emotion. A man on a horse, galloping hell-for-leather, or a man driving a pair or more of horses in like manner, a man running like an arrow from the bow, a man sailing a boat in a great gale, strikes a chord in us and is a promising subject for literary art. So would be a man flying fast through the empyrean by means of a pair of natural wings. But the man in the aeroplane or in the motor-boat or in the motor-car is somehow less inspiring—recent and fresh though he is, and eagerly waiting to have masterpieces written about him by poets and essayists and novelists. May those masterpieces be written soon! I shall welcome them the more heartily for not having expected them.

Mental speed is a thing which, like speed of limb, has always commanded admiration. We are glad that Lope de Vega wrote fifteen hundred plays. We wish our Shakespeare had done likewise, but console ourselves by the report that "he never blotted a line." It gratifies us that Father Newman wrote his lovely *Apologia* in eight weeks, and Samuel Johnson his fine *Rasselas* in the evenings of one week. We should be inspirited by any evidence that Edward Gibbon wrote the *Decline and Fall of the Roman Empire* in six months, or that Christopher Wren designed St. Paul's Cathedral in twenty-five minutes. And oh, how we should rejoice to find that the rapidity of transport that is now at our disposal had duly accelerated the pace at which our brains work! We are ashamed that our thoughts form themselves no more swiftly than in the old restful days. I have an impression that most people do talk rather faster than when I was young. They certainly eat much faster; insomuch that if I am invited to meet some of them at luncheon or dinner I find at each course that I have only just begun when they have all finished; and when I reach my home I ask, "Are there any biscuits?" Perhaps this general quickness of mastication is a sign of greater athleticism. But it may be due merely to the fact that people have so much to do now. One hears much of unemployment. But most of the people whom I meet now are employed somewhere, and after luncheon must hurry back to the places they came from. That is a very wholesome state of things. But, as a good listener, I rather sigh for the old leisurely repasts and the habit of lingering long after them to hear more from the lips of such talkers as Oscar Wilde or Henry James, Reginald Turner or Charles Brookfield—and then strolling home, well-satisfied, along the uncrowded pavements and across the quite safe roads.

Quite safe roads. Rather an arresting phrase, that! I can imagine that in more than one home some listening-in child has just exclaimed, "Oh, mother, were roads ever safe?" And perhaps the mother is at this moment telling the child that they once were—instead of listening to *me*. Perhaps she would rather *not* listen to me. Roads are a painful subject nowadays. They are railroads without rails. They are so not only in London, but all over the British Isles. They are so in every country and every city all over the world. They are places for motorists only. And the motorists themselves are not comfortable on them.

The other day, a motoristic friend of mine was complaining to me bitterly, even violently, about the behaviour of pedestrians. They were abominably careless and stupid, he insisted. I hate to see anyone agitated by a grievance, and I tried to soothe my friend by an appeal to reason. I said, "No doubt we pedestrians are very trying. But you must remember that, after all, we were on the roads for many, many centuries before you came along in your splendid car. And remember, it isn't we that are threatening to kill *you*. It is you that are threatening to kill *us*. And if we are rather flustered, and occasionally do the wrong thing, you should make allowances—and, if the worst comes to the worst, lay some flowers on our graves."

We are constantly told by the Press that we must be "traffic-conscious." But there is really no need to tell us we must be so. How could we be otherwise? How not be concussion-apprehensive, annihilation-evasive, and similar compound words? When the children of this generation, brought up in fear, shall have become adult, what sort of nervous ailments will their progeny have, one wonders? Many of the present children won't grow up at all. Very old people and very young people form the majority of those who are annually slaughtered upon our roads.

Statistics do not travel well through the air; so I shall spare you them. Nor is the air a very good vehicle for moral indignation. Tub-thumping is apt to fail there. The listener cannot see the tub, nor the fist, nor the flashing eye. But I do hope that orators on platforms are magnetically orating, all the time, about the habitual carnage; and I hope that the clergy of all denominations express themselves likewise in their pulpits, every Sunday. For I think you need rousing. You are ashamed that in years not very remote from ours young women were worked to death in the factories, and children in the coal-mines. You blush at the barbarities of criminal justice in the eighteenth and early nineteenth centuries. What do you think posterity will think of *this* age?

"Perhaps," you say, "posterity will be worse than we are." Well, then, let us set a good example to posterity. Let us persuade our legislators that we are shocked by the present state of things. Let us suggest to them that they may lose votes if they are not as shocked as we are. Let us insinuate that tests far more exacting than the present tests should be imposed on anyone who desires a licence to drive a motor-car. Let us whisper that the system by which a motorist can insure himself against any loss by his own carelessness is not a very good system. Let us, slightly raising our voices, demand that a driver convicted of dangerous driving should be liable to a much longer term of imprisonment than he is now. Let us—but all this is merely tinkering with the problem. The main root of the mischief is that great fetish of ours, Speed.

I have friends who argue brilliantly, and in perfect sincerity, that Speed in itself is no danger. They say that if the traffic were slower than it is, the number of accidents would be increased. And they quote figures, and draw diagrams, and are as able as they are technical; and I am very much bewildered. If a man said to me, "Oh, well, England is very much overpopulated," or "The Orientals don't attach the same value to life as we do; and they are notoriously wiser than we are—though they've always been so slow in comparison with us," I should understand his point of view, though I should not share it. Nor do I dispute the proposition that Speed in itself is no danger. A cannon-ball fired from a cannon is not in itself dangerous. It is dangerous only if you happen to be in the way of it. You would like to step out of its way; but there is no time for you to do so. Perhaps it would like to stop short of you; but it can't: it is going too fast. That is what motorists are doing even when in "built-up areas" they obey the speed-limit of thirty miles an hour. They are going too fast. It would be unreasonable to expect them to impose on themselves a speed-limit of twenty miles an hour. But this is the limit which should—and sooner or later will be —imposed on them. Whether this slowing-down of traffic will cause a great or a small loss of national income is, I am told, a point on which expert economists are not agreed. What is certain is that it will save annually a vast number of lives.

At first, of course, there will be much wailing and gnashing of teeth. The motorists will be frightfully sorry for themselves. And those of you who are not motorists will feel rather sorry for *them*. Rather sorry for yourselves too, perhaps. You will feel that there has been a great act of desecration: hands have been laid on the Ark of the Covenant: the divinity of Jazz has been impugned.

But here is a heartening fact for you. We are all of us travelling at a tremendous rate, and we shall always continue to do so. We shall not, it is true, be able to get rid of our speed-limit. But it is a very liberal one. 1,110 miles a minute is not a limit to be grumbled at. Our planet is not truly progressing, of course: it is back at its starting-point every year. But it never for an instant pauses in its passage through space. Nor will it do so even when, some billions of years hence, it shall have become too cold for us human beings to exist upon its surface. It will still be proceeding at its present pace: *1,110 miles a minute*.

This, Ladies and Gentlemen, is indeed a beautiful and a consoling thought—a thought for you to sleep on, to dream of. Sleep well. Dream beautifully. In fact—Good Night.

A SMALL BOY SEEING GIANTS

[SUNDAY, 26 JULY 1936]

LADIES AND GENTLEMEN, the title that has just been announced to you is perhaps rather cryptic. And as I am
not a young poet, and have not that lovely modesty which
forbids the young poet to think that his meaning could
matter twopence to anybody on this earth, I hasten to explain that the Small Boy is myself—or rather *was* myself,
half a century ago; and that the Giants were some more or
less elderly Liberal or Conservative gentlemen who gov-
erned England in those days. They were my great hobby.
I might almost say that they were my passion. I hadn't
the honour of knowing any of them personally. But I
knew them all by sight. And it was always with rapture
that I saw them.

In my earlier years, soldiers had monopolised the romantic side of me. Although, like all my coevals, I wore a

sailor suit, my heart was with the land forces; insomuch that I insisted on wearing also, out of doors, a belt with a sword attached to it, and on my breast a medal which, though it had merely the Crystal Palace embossed on it, I associated with the march to Kandahar. I used to watch with emotion the sentries changing guard outside Kensington Palace; and it was my purpose to be one of them hereafter. Meanwhile I made many feeble little drawings of them, which I coloured strongly. But somehow, mysteriously, when I was eight years old or so, the soldiery was eclipsed for me by the constabulary. Somehow the scarlet and the bearskins began to thrill me less than the austere costume and calling of the Metropolitan Police. Once in every two hours a policeman came, on his beat, past the house of my parents. At the window of the dining-room I would await his coming, punctually behold him with profound interest, and watch him out of sight. It was not the daffodils that marked for me the coming of the season of Spring. It was the fact that policemen suddenly wore short tunics with steel buttons. It was not the fall of the leaf nor the swallows' flight that signalled Autumn to me. It was the fact that policemen were wearing long thick frock-coats with buttons of copper. But even more than in the day-time did policemen arrest me, as it were, in the watches of the night. The dark lantern was the truly great, the irresistible thing about them. More than once, from the window of my night-nursery, I had seen that lantern flashed at opposite front doors and through area-railings. My paintings of policemen were mostly nocturnes—a dim, helmeted figure with a long white ray of light. Although I possessed, of course, a dark lantern of my own, and used it much, I preferred my occasional glimpses of the genuine article, and looked forward impatiently to being a member of the Force. But the young are faithless. By the time I was eleven years old I despised the Force. I was interested only in politicians—in Statesmen, as they were called at that time.

I had already, for some years, been aware of them. I had seen them, two-dimensionally and on a small scale, every Wednesday, in the pages of *Punch*, and had in a remote and tepid way revered them. I had not thought of them as actual, live men. Rather, they were, as portrayed in the cartoons of the great John Tenniel, nobly mythical to me. Sometimes they wore togas; but more often they wore chitons and breast-plates, and were wielding or brandishing swords. Their shins were protected by greaves, and their calves were immensely muscular; and in the matter of biceps they were unsurpassable. They were Ajaxes and Hectors and Achilleses. Now and then they rose to greater heights, becoming Herculeses, Vulcans, Marses, and the like. *Punch* was firmly Gladstonian in its politics; and therefore the Prime Minister was always more muscular than any of his enemies, redoubtable though they too were; and the attitudes that he struck were more striking than theirs. I didn't quite like this. For my father was a Conservative, and so, accordingly, was I. I wished—though I didn't care enough to pray—for the downfall of Gladstone. Some time in the year 1883 I read a speech delivered in the House of Commons by Lord Randolph Churchill. I felt that here was the man to compass the downfall; for he was so very rude. Even the best-behaved little boys rejoice in the rudeness of other people. Lord Randolph's rudeness in a good cause refreshed my young heart greatly; nor ever did his future speeches disappoint me. But, much though I delighted in him, I didn't quite think of him as an actual person. I thought of him as Phaëton. Tenniel—or was it Linley Sambourne?—had depicted him as Phaëton, standing ready on the ground while old Sir Stafford Northcote (the leader of the Opposition, here depicted as Phoebus Apollo) was driving the chariot of the sun. I resented the cartoonist's analogy. But the physical image abode with me.

It was the London Stereoscopic Company that first opened my eyes to the fact that Churchill and Gladstone, Northcote and Harcourt, Chamberlain, Hartington, and all those others were actual, mortal, modern men. Not until I was nearly twelve did I inspect that great long double window on the eastern side of Regent Street, famous for its galaxy of photographs of eminent personages. The place of honour was accorded of course to members of the Royal Family. But precedence over Archbishops and Bishops, Generals, Admirals, Poets, Actors and Actresses, was taken by the Statesmen, as we no longer call them. Not even to Lord Tennyson and Sir Garnet Wolseley and Mr. Henry Irving and Miss Connie Gilchrist was accorded such prominence as to the least of these. For these were giants in those days. They were not perhaps Gods, but they certainly were Titans, in the public eye. And here they all were in *my* eye, tailored and hosier'd as men. With luck, I might some day see one of them in the street. I studied the portraits keenly. I fixed the features in my mind. I stayed there long. And on my way home I saw a man who was unmistakably—Mr. Childers. To you, Ladies and Gentlemen, I suppose his name means nothing. But he was at that time Chancellor of the Exchequer. It was a great, a throbbing moment.

Of Mr. Childers I made several drawings—very unpromising little drawings—when I reached my home. And thereafter, in the course of my holidays from school, I drew many of his colleagues. When a Cabinet Council was to be held, the fact was usually announced by the morning papers of that day. And there at the hour appointed, there on the pavement of Downing Street, opposite to No. 10, would be I, awaiting breathlessly the advent of the Giants. The greatest and most awful of them all would of course be invisible. Mr. Gladstone was somewhere behind those brown brick walls. But the others would be vouchsafed to me, one of them coming perhaps from the direction of Parliament Street, another from the courtyard of the Government Offices behind me, another up the flight of steps from St. James's Park. They are dead, one and all of them. Most of them died very many years ago. While I stood staring at them, Mr. Asquith was unknown to them: he was just a barrister in fairly good practice. The present Father of the House of Commons, Mr. Lloyd George, was a young solicitor, roaming nightly with bare feet and dreamful eyes along the clouded ridges of the Welsh mountains and hailing the roseate dawn. Mr. Baldwin was at Harrow. A quite recent President of the Oxford Union, Mr. George Nathaniel Curzon, was travelling observantly in the waste spaces of Siam and of Korea. Mr. Edward Carson was just beginning to make a name for himself in the Irish police-courts. Mr. Austen Chamberlain was at Trinity College, Cambridge. Mr. Neville Chamberlain was at Rugby. Mr. Winston Churchill was a pugnacious and not very happy little boy at a preparatory school. Many, many years were to elapse before Mr. Duff Cooper and Mr. Anthony Eden, Mr. Harold Nicolson and Mr. A. P. Herbert, were summoned forth from among the infinite ranks of the unborn. I am what the writers of obituary notices call "an interesting link with the past."

I wish I could have foreseen the future. Had I done so —had I known how exactly, how furtively like one another our rulers would try to look—I should have revelled even more than I did revel at the sight of those men of 1884. Visually, they let themselves go, without self-consciousness or fear. Each one of them was a law unto himself. Some of them—Lord Kimberley, for example, and Mr. Dodson—had beards without moustaches. Some of them were clean-shaven. One of them, Mr. Shaw-Lefevre, had always what looked like a four days' growth of beard. Lord Hartington's beard and moustache were far longer than Sir Charles Dilke's. Mr. Joseph Chamberlain was content with small side-whiskers. Sir William Harcourt had a "Newgate frill." So had Lord Northbrook, who wore, however and moreover, a becoming tuft on the chin. The wide, pale, pleasantly roguish face of old Lord Granville was framed in masses of silvery curls. Some wore their hair long, others short. Some of them dressed badly, others—in an off-hand way—well. To none of them except Chamberlain and Dilke, those two harbingers of another age, would one have applied the epithet *neat*. Believe me, they offered no end of latitude to the limner.

Spiritually, nevertheless, they bore strong likenesses to one another. Barring the two harbingers, and barring of course Mr. Gladstone, who was a creature apart, not to be fitted into any category whatsoever, they were authentic Whigs, one and all; eighteenth-century men, despite their date. Some of them were old enough to have dined, often, at Holland House. Not one of them, I feel sure, had failed to breakfast frequently with Mr. Samuel Rogers. The new Government Offices were still new to them, and I expect they admired those buildings greatly. They remembered the time when Downing Street had lodging-houses in it, and a tavern or two, and a milliner's shop—things inconsonant with the affairs of a great nation. I daresay they regretted that Nos. 10 and 11 had not been demolished and rebuilt in the grandiose modern fashion. What charm would the eighteenth century have had for gentlemen who were a part of it? The love of by-gone things is a quite recent growth—due mainly to the fact that we have fallen on evil times. If we could all of us follow Mr. H. G. Wells's good example, dismiss the present from our minds, and fix our eyes steadfastly in the future, then we could share his wholesome contempt for the past. But we can't. We are morbid. I, perhaps, more so than most of us. Some weeks ago, as I was passing through St. James's Park, I looked up towards the street that I had so fondly haunted in my childhood—the street of the Giants. I ascended the steps to it and stood again before No. 10, gazing. "This sweet corner" Horace Walpole had called it in a letter written by him therefrom to Sir Horace Mann. "Sweet" is a trivial epithet, but one must remember that Horace's father, Sir Robert, had no preceding Giant in that corner: only a little of history had been made there as yet; the rest was to come. I gazed at the house of Pitt and Palmerston, Disraeli, Gladstone, and all those others; at the narrow front-door, with the unassuming fanlight above it; at the lantern in the traceries of the wrought-iron "overthrow" beneath which so many Giants had stepped so long before I was born. And then my eye was attracted by a grey-blue placard in one of the two hall-windows. I crossed the road to read it. . . .

GARDEN PARTY
MRS. STANLEY BALDWIN
AT HOME
AT NO. 10, DOWNING STREET
IN AID OF
THE SAFER MOTHERHOOD APPEAL
TUESDAY JULY 14
WHEN THE WORLD'S GREATEST
MALE ENSEMBLE OF 35 PERFORMERS
THE DON COSSACK CHOIR
WITH THEIR FAMOUS CONDUCTOR
SERGE JAROFF
WILL MAKE THEIR ONE APPEARANCE IN LONDON THIS
SEASON
TICKETS £2. 2. 0.

These words I read with surprise, but with entire sympathy. Here was an excellent cause to support, a very good use for the old garden to be put to. Had I been rich enough, I would have bought a ticket. But I rather wondered what Horace Walpole would have had to say in the matter. Something supercilious, something flippant, I am afraid. He was rather inhuman.

I wished I could see again those old Gladstonian figures —and the Salisburyans who succeeded to them in '85: the distinguished and formidable figure of Sir Michael Hicks-Beach; the distinguished and venerable figure of Lord John Manners, that last survivor of the Young England movement, whom Miss Charlotte Brontë, when as a young man he visited Haworth parsonage, had thought so handsome; above all, the distinguished and attractive figure of Lord Randolph, my chosen hero. He seemed, in some ways, always rather out of the picture. He seemed young for Downing Street, and had the air of a man of fashion rather than of affairs. He alone wore a moustache without beard or whiskers—an arrangement suggestive of levity. His was the only top hat that was ironed, and it was ironed to the utmost lustre. He alone smoked cigarettes, and he smoked them through a very long amber mouthpiece. He, and only he, sometimes wore a buttonhole. Sometimes he looked as happy and insouciant as Mr. Gladstone's young disciple, Lord Rosebery; at other times, and oftener, he looked as tragically sad as did Lord Rosebery in later years. Very different though the two men were in character, they had points in common. The gods had bestowed on both of them shining gifts of mind and of speech, and had foredoomed them both to fail irretrievably.

There is much to be said for failure. It is more interesting than success. Rosebery and Randolph Churchill are, among the office-holders of their generation, the only two that still hold our attention and stir our curiosity. Lord Salisbury, their elder contemporary, is a noble, a monumental figure which does not detain us. It may be that if the veteran Mr. Gladstone had carried Home Rule he would be rather less detentive than he now is. For some time after his death we tended to depreciate him. Three or four years ago I was amused by a conversation between two political ladies of fashion, one an Asquithian Liberal, the other a Tory. The Liberal one, after having spoken of

Mr. Gladstone with enthusiasm, said, "But of course people only talk of Dizzy now. Gladstone's forgotten." The Tory one said, "Oh—I thought he was rather comin' in again, dear?" She was right. Mr. Gladstone is once more with us. Here he is, the mystical realist. Dizzy, the sceptical idealist, is rather further away. Dizzy is, of course— Dizzy always was—irresistible. His novels, his phrases, some of his speeches even, can still delight us deeply. His imagination and his wit are glorious, as was his patience. But he lacks something. In the last year of his life, speaking to one of the members of the Fourth Party, he said, "I fully appreciate your feelings, but you must stick to Northcote. He represents the respectability of the Party. I wholly sympathise with you all, because *I* was never respectable." Nor has he become so. We can revel in him; but we cannot respect him. There is something unreal, something absurd about him. In this unrestful and threatened age of the world's history we are moved to hanker after the moral force and fervour, and the endless vitality of Gladstone. We want a Gladstone *de nos jours*.

I saw him only three times. Once from the Strangers' Gallery in the House of Commons, early in 1885; and then and there, for the first and last time, I also heard him. He was merely answering a question about procedure, but he spoke for not less than a couple of minutes, in low tones, leaning far forward, with hands outspread upon the table, and ever turning from side to side and around, envisaging the whole assembly. Though I regarded him as a great power for evil, he fascinated, he won me. The second time was a year or so later. I was one of the crowd that assembled in Parliament Square when he was about to introduce the first Home Rule Bill. There were boos among the cheers as he drove past, beside his wife, in an open landau, gravely bowing, his great dark eyes very wide open in his ivory-white old face. I was not among the booers. I cheered—in spite of myself—wildly. The third time, I was an undergraduate, standing on the steps outside the Sheldonian Theatre, in which building Mr. Gladstone, after long absence from Oxford, was to lecture on the Homeric poems. The Vice-Chancellor's brougham punctually arrived, and out of it stepped the Vice-Chancellor and, in his D.C.L. robes, Mr. Gladstone, bareheaded, amidst a tumultuous welcome. He ascended the steps, dark-eyed, white-faced, smiling; very old, but stalwart; he turned, stood, bowed slowly, deeply, from side to side, to the crowd below. He had bowed to many crowds, in his day, but never to one that loved him more than this one. I associate him always with Oxford.

And it was with Oxford—more, even, than with Scotland, I think—that he especially associated himself. When he lay dying, the Hebdomadal Council sent to him a message of regard and affection. "To this," says his biographer, John Morley, "he listened most attentively and over it brooded long, then he dictated to his youngest daughter sentence by sentence his reply: 'There is no expression of Christian sympathy that I could value more than that of the ancient University of Oxford, the God-fearing and God-sustaining University of Oxford. I served her, perhaps mistakenly, but to the best of my ability. My most earnest prayers are with her to the uttermost and to the last.' "

These are grand words. With them let me close my discourse. I said at the outset that I was an interesting link with the past. Perhaps that was begging the question. I claim merely that I am a link with the past. If I have bored you, forgive me. And be of good cheer. This is the last time that I shall have the honour of addressing you, for the present. I am going to Italy, to my home, and shall not soon be here again. And so I wish you not only Goodnight, but also Goodbye.

MUSIC HALLS OF MY YOUTH

[Sunday, 18 January 1942]

Ladies and Gentlemen, or—if you prefer that mode of address—G'deevning.

It is past my bed-time; for when one is very old one reverts to the habits of childhood, and goes to bed quite early—though not quite so early as one went to one's night-nursery; and not by command, but just of one's own accord, without any kicking or screaming. I always hear the nine o'clock news and the postscript; but soon after these I am in bed and asleep. I take it that my few elders and most of my contemporaries will have switched off and retired ere now, and that you who are listening to me are either in the prime of life or in the flush of enviable youth, and will therefore know little of the subject on which I am going to dilate with senile garrulity.

Would that those others had sat up to hear me! In them

(36)

I could have struck the fond, the vibrant chords of memory. To instruct is a dreary function. I should have liked to thrill, to draw moisture to the eyes. But, after all, you do, all of you, know *something* of my theme. The historic sense bloweth where it listeth, and in the past few years there has been a scholarly revival of interest in the kind of melodies which I had supposed were to lie in eternal oblivion. Some forty years ago that enlightened musician, Cecil Sharp, was ranging around remote parts of England and coaxing eldest inhabitants in ingle-nooks to quaver out folk-songs that only they remembered. It was a great good work that Cecil Sharp did in retrieving for us so many beautiful old tunes and poems—poems and tunes in which are enshrined for us a happier and better life than ours, a life lived under the auspices of Nature. I salute his memory. And I take leave to think that he would have been as glad—well, almost as glad—as I am to hear often, on the wireless, revocations of things warbled across the footlights of Music Halls in decades long ago. For these too are folk-songs, inalienably English, and racy of—no, not of the soil, but of the pavements from which they sprang. I even take leave to think that if Shakespeare had lived again and had heard them warbled in the Halls he might have introduced them into his plays, just as he had introduced—with magical variations, of course—the folk-songs of his own time. He might have done so. Or again, he might *not*. For he was very keen, poor man, on a thing which many of the younger poets of our day disapprove of, as being in rather bad taste: the element of beauty. And I cannot claim that this element was to be found in the songs of the "Lion Comique" or of the "Serio" of my day, or of the days before mine. Indeed,

I cannot claim for these ditties much more than that there was in them a great gusto. But gusto is an immense virtue. Gusto goes a huge long way.

"My day," as I have called it, dawned exactly fifty-one years ago. I was a callow undergraduate, in my first Christmas vacation. I had been invited to dine at the Café Royal by my brother Julius, whose age was twice as great as mine; and after dinner he proposed that we should go to the Pavilion Music Hall, where a man called Chevalier had just made his debut, and had had a great success. I was filled with an awful, but pleasant, sense of audacity in venturing into such a place, so plebeian and unhallowed a den, as a Music Hall; and I was relieved, though slightly disappointed also, at finding that the Pavilion seemed very like a theatre, except that the men around us were mostly smoking, and not in evening clothes, and that there was alongside of the stalls an extensive drinking-bar, of which the barmaids were the only—or almost the only—ladies present, and that the stage was occupied by one man only. One and only, but great: none other than The Great Mac-Dermott, of whom I had often heard in my childhood as the singer of "We Don't Want to Fight, But, By Jingo, If We *Do*." And here he was, in the flesh, in the grease-paint, surviving and thriving, to my delight; a huge old burly fellow, with a yellow wig and a vast expanse of crumpled shirt-front that had in the middle of it a very large, not *very* real diamond stud. And he was still belligerent, wagging a great imperative forefinger at us across the footlights, and roaring in a voice slightly husky but still immensely powerful a song with the refrain "That's What We'd Like to Do!" In Russia there had been repressive measures against Nihilists, and Mr. Joseph Hatton had

written a book entitled *By Order of the Czar*—a book that
created a great sensation. And in consequence of it the
Great MacDermott had been closeted with the Prime Minister; nor did he treat the interview as confidential. I remember well some words of his song.

" 'What would you like to do, my Lord?'
    I asked Lord Salisburee"—

but the words need the music; and I remember the music
quite well too. A pity I can't sing it. But perhaps I could
do a croaking suggestion of it. . . .

(*Sung*) " 'What would you like to do, my Lord?'
    I asked Lord Salisburee.
'The great Election's very near,
    And where will then you be?
The English people have the right
    To fight for those who are
Being oppressed and trodden down
    By Order of the Czar.
That's what we'd like to do!
    Beware lest we do it too!
To join those aspirants
    Who'd crush Russian tyrants—
That's what we'd like to do!' "

And I do assure you that the audience would have liked to
do it. You may wonder at that, after hearing my voice.
You would not have wondered had you heard the Great
MacDermott's.

But the fierce mood was short-lived. There arose in the

firmament another luminary. Albert Chevalier, as new as MacDermott was old, came shining forth amidst salvoes of fervid expectation. A very elastic and electric little creature, with twists and turns of face and body and voice as many as the innumerable pearl buttons that adorned his jacket and his breeches. Frankly fantastic, but nevertheless very real, very human and loveable in his courtship of 'Arriet by moonlight, or in his enjoyment of the neighbours' good wishes as he drove his little donkey-chaise along the Old Kent Road. I was at that time too young to appreciate the subtleties of the technique that he had acquired and matured on the legitimate stage. But in later years I knew enough to realise that he was becoming rather a slave to these subtleties. He was no longer content to merge his acting in the singing of a song. He acted outside the song, acted at leisure between the notes, letting lilt and rhythm go to the deuce. But his composition of words and music never became less good. There was always a firm basic idea, a clear aspect of human character. "My Old Dutch," "The Little Nipper," "You Can't Get a Roise out o' Oi," and the rest of them, still live for that reason. I had the pleasure of meeting him once, in his later years, and was sorely tempted to offer him an idea which might well have been conceived by himself: a song about a publican whom the singer had known and revered, who was now dead, whose business was carried on by his son, Ben, an excellent young man,—"But 'e'll never be the man 'is Father woz." The chorus was to be something of this sort:

> (*Sung*) "I drops in to see young Ben
> In 'is tap-room now an' then,

And I likes to see 'im gettin' on becoz
'E's got pluck and 'e's got brains,
And 'e takes no end o' pains,
But—'e'll never be the man 'is Father woz."

But nothing so irks a creative artist as to be offered an idea, good or bad. And I did not irk Chevalier.

A man who introduces into an art-form a new style of his own has usually to pay a high price for having done so. Imitators crop up on all sides, cheapening his effects. This price Chevalier did not have to pay. He escaped in virtue of being partly French. His manner and method were inimitable in our rough island Halls. Singers of coster songs began to abound, but they were thoroughly native and traditional. Gus Elen defied the conventions only by the extreme, the almost desperate glumness of his demeanour, and the bitterness of what he had to say, on a stage where cheeriness against all odds was ever the resounding key-note. Immensely acrid was the spirit of his " 'E Dunno Where 'E Are" and of his "Well, It's a Grite Big Shime"; but even these were mild in comparison with the withering pessimism of a later song of his. Often in reading the work of some of those younger poets whom I have mentioned I am reminded of that other famous song, "What's the good of ennyfink? Why, nuffink!"

Very different was the philosophy of Dan Leno. Fate had not smiled on him, his path was a hard one, he was beset by carking troubles and anxieties, he was all but at his wits' end, the shadow of the workhouse loomed, but there was in his little breast a passion of endurance, and a constant fount of hope, that nothing could subdue. His meagre face was writhen with care, but the gleam in his eyes proclaimed him undefeatable. He never asked for sympathy: he had too much of Cockney pride to do that; but the moment he appeared on the stage our hearts were all his. Nature had made him somehow irresistible. Nor do I remember any one so abundant in drollery of patter. He was, by the way, the inaugurator of patter. In his later years he hardly sang at all. There was just a perfunctory gabble of a stanza and a chorus, and the rest was a welter of the spoken word—and of imaginative genius.

He used to appear yearly in the Drury Lane panto-mime, with the enormous Herbert Campbell as foil to him. But there he was wasted. Team-work nullified him. He could shine only in detachment. Besides, Drury Lane was too big for anybody but Herbert Campbell; and for him, it seemed to me, any Music Hall was too small. But I was very fond of him, that Boanergetic interpreter of the old tradition, with Mr. James Fawn as his only peer or rival. Physically somewhat less great than these two, Mr. Charles Godfrey had a wider range. He could be heroic as well as comic; and he abounded also in deep sentiment. "After the Ball" is indeed a classic; but alas, as I found some years ago in a modern song-book, the text has been corrupted, to suit tastes less naïve than ours were. The un-sophisticated syntax of what Godfrey sang in his baggy dress-suit has been wantonly changed. No doubt you know the opening words of the present version. But what Godfrey gave us was

> (*Sung*) "Came a small maiden,
>   Climbed on my knees,
>   'Tell me a story,
>   Do, Uncle, please!'

> 'Tell you a story?
> What shall I tell?
> Tales about giants?
> Or in the dell?'
> After the Ball was over,
> After the"—

and so on. But "Tales about giants? Or in the dell?" That's the thing to remember and cherish.

Mr. Harry Freeman, dear man, sounded no depths, and scaled no heights of sentiment, and indeed had no pretensions of any kind, except a thorough knowledge of his business, which was the singing of songs about Beer, about the Lodger, about being had up before the Beak, about the Missus, about the sea-side, and all the other safest and surest themes. He never surprised one. He never disappointed one. He outstood in virtue of being a perfect symbol and emblem of the average. I delighted in him deeply. I think he had a steadying influence on me. To this day, whenever I am over-excited, or am tempted to take some unusual and unwise course, I think of Harry Freeman.

A saliently sharp antithesis to him was R. G. Knowles, surnamed "The Very Peculiar American Comedian." Nothing restful, everything peculiar, about *him!* He alone had a "signature tune." He was the inventor of that asset. The opening bars of Mendelssohn's Wedding March were played as he rushed on from the wings, hoarsely ejaculating "I've only a moment to linger with you": a tall man with a rather scholarly face, wearing a very shabby frock-coat, an open collar, and not very white duck trousers, much frayed at the heels of very large old boots; also an opera-hat, flat-brimmed and tilted far back from the brow. He spoke rather huskily, with a strong native twang, at the rate of about ten words to the second. I tremble to think how many anecdotes he must always have uttered before he broke into a brief song and rushed away to linger for a moment with an audience in one of the other Halls. From some of his anecdotes one gathered that he was no prude. But there one wronged him. Some years ago my dear friend William Archer, the famous dramatic critic, and introducer of Ibsen to our shores, told me that he had recently met, travelling in India, a man of whom I probably knew a good deal, R. G. Knowles, a Music Hall performer. "He told me," said Archer, "that he had definitely retired from the Music Halls; and I asked him why. He said that the tone of them had fallen to a very low level: there was so much that was ob-jectionable. He said, 'Mr. Archer, in *my* turns there was never anything ob-jectionable. Sudge-estive—*yes.*' "

I am not in a position to deny that ob-jectionability may have supervened. I had ceased to attend the Halls because the virus of "Variety" had come creeping in: conjurors, performing elephants, tramp-bicyclists, lightning calculators, and so on, and so forth. The magic had fled —the dear old magic of the unity—the monotony, if you will—of song after song after song, good, bad, and indifferent, but all fusing one with another and cumulatively instilling a sense of deep beatitude—a strange sweet foretaste of Nirvana.

I often wondered, in the old Tivoli and elsewhere, who wrote the common ruck of the songs I was listening to, and what the writers bought one half so precious as the wares they sold. As to their tariff, I once had a queer little sidelight on that in a newspaper report of a case in the County Court at Hastings. The defendant stated that he earned his living by writing the words and music for Music Hall songs. He was asked by the Judge how much he earned in the course of a year. He replied promptly, "Three hundred and sixty-five pounds." And then, the Judge being astonished at such exactitude, he explained that he was paid one pound for every song, and wrote one every day.

I should have liked to learn more about him. That he was not of the straitest sect of Sabbatarians is obvious. For the rest, what manner of man was he? Was he entirely a creature of habit? Or had he sometimes to plod without aid from his Muse, while at other times she showered inspiration on him? Was it in the comic or in the sentimental vein that he was happier? And was he a discerning judge of his own work? For aught I know, he may have written and composed "Daisy, Daisy, Give Me Your Answer True." On the evening of that day, did he say to himself, "Not marble nor the gilded monuments of princes shall outlive this powerful rhyme?" And this question leads to another. Why, exactly, has "Daisy, Daisy" triumphed perennially, holding her ground against all comers? There is a reason for everything in this world, there is a solution of every mystery. And, with your co-operation, I should like to—but time forbids. I should like also to have said a great deal about Marie Lloyd, whose funeral was less impressive only than that of the great Duke of Wellington; about Little Tich, who took Paris by storm; about Vesta Tilley and Mark Sheridan; also about Miss Ada Reeve, and about Mr. George Robey. To her, and to him, and to the shades of those others, I apologise for my silence. The work of all of them gave me great delight in my youth. Perhaps you will blame me for having spent so much of my time in Music Halls, so frivolously, when I should have been sticking to my books, burning the midnight oil and compassing the larger latitude. But I am impenitent. I am inclined to think, indeed I have always thought, that a young man who desires to know all that in all ages in all lands has been thought by the best minds, and wishes to make a synthesis of all those thoughts for the future benefit of mankind, is laying up for himself a very miserable old age.

Good night, childrenn. . . .

ADVERTISEMENTS

LADIES AND GENTLEMEN, I am afraid my subject is rather an exciting one; and as I don't like excitement I shall approach it in a gentle, timid, round-about way. I am all for a quiet life. That is a deplorable confession, I suppose. I remember that many people were irritated and reproachful when, as a youngish man, I wrote in some newspaper, or in some book, that my ideal of happiness was "a four-post bed in a field of poppies and mandragora." London, when I wrote those words, was not so large a city as it has since become, but it was too large, and too civic, for my taste, and great always was my pleasure in getting away from it, for a while, whenever I could: away from the hustle and the jostle that ought to have been so congenial to me.

In 1910, when I was thirty-seven years old, I did alto-

gether get away from it, to a little house on a coast-road
of the Gulf of Genoa. A very quiet coast-road, traversed
mostly by rustic carts and horses; a road on which a
motor-car created excitement; a road on which little children ran races during a great part of the day. But a foreign
country in war-time—however friendly to one's cause—
is an uncomforting place to be in. One wants to be where
the English language is spoken, and English thoughts and
feelings are expressed. Early in 1915 I was back in England, for rather more than the duration of what we in-
genuously called the Great War. In the years that followed, considerable strides were being made along the
aforesaid coast-road towards modern civilisation. The
road itself was magnificently asphalted from side to side;
the carts and horses were fewer than before; but great
plenty of motor-cars and motor-bicycles more than
atoned for this fewness; and the heartiness of their hoot-
ing and of their mostly open exhausts was a great im-
provement on the cries of those little boys and little girls
who had been wont to run races, and could no longer do
so. . . . I wish, Ladies and Gentlemen, I could cure myself of the habit of speaking ironically. I should so like to
express myself in a quite straightforward manner. But
perhaps it's as well that I can't; for, if I could, my language might be over-strong for Sunday evening.

It is now four years since the darkening omens of another war brought me once more to England. Since then
London has become a far quieter city, by day and by
night, than it was in my youth, and an infinitely quieter
one than it presently became; and now, when I come up
to it from the country, I do not experience the shock with
which it used to assail me. And I should feel thankful for

the change if the reason for it were not so tragic a one. Or should I? A quiet capital city is a contradiction in terms. It is a thing uncanny, spectral. London is quiet for the first time in its history. I imagine that it never was noisier than in the seething days of the Elizabethans. In the eighteenth century life had become more or less canalised, the social structure had taken rigid shape. But Horace Walpole and the characters in *The School for Scandal*—barring Charles Surface—were not typical of the time. It was rather Charles's time than Joseph's or Horace's: a robust and loud time. The Regency was an age of din, and the din did not immediately die down in Early Victorian times. It was modified only later by the coming in of the great new middle class, a class that was not, like the nobility and the mob, sure of itself. This slight lull ceased in the Edvardian Era—an era which began many years before the death of Queen Victoria and lasted for four years after King Edward's death; an era that was in its social manifestations very like to the Second Empire in France. Perhaps some young man who is listening to me has often thought he would like to have lived in Edvardian days. I myself, when I was young, had a hankering after the Second Empire. I never realised that it was here and now—and I not enjoying it. Imagination is a great painter and gilder, is she not?

Of London in the period between the last war and this one I saw little; but I gather from what I have heard and read—from things said and written by quite good-natured, non-censorious people—that it is not a period of which one has great reason to feel, on the whole, proud. What I saw of it for myself seemed to me a distinctly inferior imitation of the Edvardian model. That model had not been altogether without grace. It assuredly had not lacked gusto. These qualities seemed to me rather lacking in the revival. But the noisiness was undeniably, I thought, greater. And the kind of noisiness that had increased more than any other was that visible kind which is especially unbeloved by me. There had been an horrific increase in the volume, the torrential spate and flood of— advertisements.

Those waters have now, of course, subsided very much; they are comparatively a trickle. But I presume that after this war, if economic conditions permit, they will rise again in all their diluvian and submersive strength. Even now they are no mere trickle as compared with what they were in my childhood. And I confess to a fondness for the memory of those which found their way into my nursery. There was a fruit-salt of which I have since been told by experts that the proprietor was the Father of Modern Advertising. If indeed he was so, he, that dear old quiet man, builded greater than he knew. There was nothing startling, nothing arresting in his writings. They weren't even terse. They were by way of being prolix, and were interspersed with quotations from the Old Testament, and with references to anything that came into his head; and they were printed in very small, closely set, unassuming type. But I read them carefully, with all the pride of one who had but lately learned to read. And my fancy was always engaged by the accompanying rather smudgy woodcut at the top of the column. I clearly remember the look of radiant well-being which not even the smudginess could disguise on the faces of the grandfather, the grandmother, the mother, the father, and the children seated round a lamp-lit table with a turkey or a plum-pudding—or was it both?—in the midst of them. And there was a similar family eating its Christmas dinner out of doors, in the rays of the sun, in Australia. This struck a deep geographical chord of wonder in my little breast. Somewhat later, a wonderful soap swam into my ken. Sir John Millais had painted a great picture of a little boy with golden curls and a green velveteen suit, and upturned eyes, blowing bubbles; and this picture had been acquired by the vendor of the soap and widely reproduced on the soap's behalf. My elders, in those pre-historic days, wondered that Sir John should have authorised this use of his great gifts. And they were shocked, too, that the beautiful young Mrs. Langtry had for the soap's sake allowed engravings of a photograph of herself to be sown broadcast in the Press, with the admonition "For look you, she is fair as a lily!" Mrs. Weldon, the famous litigant, had gone even further. Her portrait was subscribed by her, "I am forty-seven, but my complexion is seventeen." I wonder what my elders would think of those perfectly well-brought-up and non-litigious young ladies of rank and fashion who nowadays let their photographs be reproduced in favour of some unguent used by them and ecstatically praised by them, with an accompanying diagram of their features and a laudatory description of each feature by the unguentarian?

Only fools, of course, would accuse these young ladies of advertising themselves. They passionately believe in this or that balm and cannot but testify to the faith that is in them. But fools are not few in this world, and I rather wish the young ladies belonged to some guild that forbade its members to do anything that might be misconstrued as a desire for personal publicity. There is such a guild for doctors, another for barristers, another for stockbrokers, as we all know. Perhaps in course of time the Medical

Council and the Bar Council and the Committee of the Stock Exchange will be broader-minded and more indulgent—who knows? Meanwhile their members are implacably debarred from advertising in the Press, and never do so. And yet, no, even as I speak these words, I remember —or rather even as I wrote these words to be read to you I remembered—an advertisement by a doctor, a very concise and therefore not expensive one, that caught my eye many years ago in *The Church Times:* "Medical Man in Cheltenham can accommodate one female resident patient. Epileptic Churchwoman preferred." This pleased me much; and of course there was nothing in it that could pain the Medical Council. The doctor did not give his name—gave merely his initials and "Box" such and such a number; and he promised no cure at all. But perhaps he was the thin end of the wedge?

To these "Want" advertisements, as I think they are called, to these spontaneous cries from the heart, I have no objection at all. It is the "You *do* want, and woe betide if you don't get" ones that bore me to death. We are taught to believe that the outcriers are entirely altruistic men. Some years ago there was held at Wembley an International Advertising Convention, which lasted for three days or so. I was not present, but the speeches made at it were very fully reported in all the organs of the daily Press. And I gathered that the Advertisers were very noble fellows indeed. They were spending themselves in what they called Service. The hall in which they met was adorned with strenuously edifying slogans: "All for Each, and Each for All" is the one that I best remember. I gathered that these proprietors and these agents of theirs were not "out," as they would have said, to make a good deal of money. Their aim, their incentive was just to serve you and me, to irradiate our darkness and give us full and happy lives. They spoke not as tradesmen; they spake as Crusaders, as Knights of the Holy Grail. I rather wondered they hadn't had a marching-song composed for them. They ought to have come tramping from Wembley to London, four abreast, under flying banners, chanting a song with that almost sacred refrain: "All for Each and Each for All." I am sorry to say that I presently struck a jarring note. I was having an exhibition of caricatures at the Leicester Galleries; and one of these, hung in the middle of one of the walls, was a group of strong, stout, square-jawed business-men, with hands piously folded and brass haloes attached to their heads, and with a very rude inscription by me beneath them. I have often wondered who bought the nefarious thing. I am sorry to say that on the opening day it was one of the first drawings sold. It was described in two papers, *The Manchester Guardian* and *The Saturday Review*: the others drew over it the veil of pained silence.

Who was it—Lord Macaulay, I think—who first called the Press the Fourth Estate of the Realm? The advertisers are now certainly the Fifth. "As you are strong," I venture to say to them, "be merciful. Do try not to be quite so strong here as you are in, for instance, America." I have seen American weekly and monthly magazines in which at first glance it isn't easy to find anything *but* advertisements. All the rest is printed in disjected fragments. An essay or a story begins briefly, say, on page 20, and then you must turn to page 33, and thence to page 47, amidst the glare and blare of things for sale. And in the London daily papers how much less space than of yore can be spared, could even before the war be spared, for consideration of the arts of literature, drama, painting, music—or even for the utterances of senators. Of course the advertisers are not really to blame, nor are the editors. The mischief is due to the enormous increase in the cost of producing a newspaper. The cost of book-production has, I suppose, gone up not less hideously. But so far the pages of novels or poems, of essays or biographies, have not been interspersed by their publishers with paeans on the various competing brands of whisky and millinery and cigarettes. Perhaps, after we have won the war, not even *this* mercy will be vouchsafed to us. Meanwhile, if I were endowed with wealth, I should start a great advertising campaign in all the principal newspapers. The advertisements would consist of one short sentence, printed in huge block letters—a sentence that I once heard spoken by a husband to a wife: "My dear, nothing in this world is worth buying." But of course I should alter "my dear" to "my dears."

And now for a matter which agitates me far more than the effect that advertisements have on newspapers. Though newspapers without advertisements could not nowadays survive, I see no reason for believing that without this support the streets and squares of our cities, and the roads and hills and valleys of our countryside, would presently disappear. On the contrary, they are rather by way of disappearing already behind the insistences on what we ought to purchase. Beautiful architecture and beautiful scenery are things far more important to the soul of man than even the best newspaper. So too is the sky, surely; especially the sky by night. But the advertisers are creatures of the night as well as of the day.

Some years ago, a clever man invented a device by which illuminated advertisements could be inscribed upon the sky by night and would remain fixed there for a fairly long time. The sanction of Parliament was somehow necessary to the execution of this plan. There was strong opposition to it from many quarters, certainly from all the best ones. But the Bill, with some slight modification, was passed by both Houses. That beautiful quarter of London, the Adelphi, had recently been handed over by them for demolition and for skyscrapers. Why *shouldn't* the sky be scraped? And why shouldn't it have advertisements scrawled on it? Is this a free country, or is it not? What right have its rulers to prevent *anybody* from making money wherever he sees a chance of doing so? To hinder him, thought the majority of Lords and Commons, would be un-English. Some of them perhaps went even further, and thought that it wouldn't be cricket.

But the invention seems not to have fulfilled its dreadful promise. So far as I know, the space between us and the stars remained unmolested, and all was well. And now, during this war we can further be glad of one thing: that London by night is not vulgarised and debased by those loathsome red-hot-coal illuminations, appearing and clumsily spelling themselves out and disappearing and re-appearing on the coping and façades of buildings. If such things must be, let them be done with some semblance of taste and fancy. Many of you will have seen and rather liked, in this and that foreign city, those inscriptions in neon light on the frontages of shops by night: inscriptions done in graceful, fluent lettering, and in pleasant tints—primrose, or pale pink, or lavender. But in the average foreign country there is a Ministry of Fine Arts, and to that Ministry all such spectacular advertisements must be submitted, and by it approved. We ourselves nowadays have a Ministry of almost everything. Some day perhaps we shall have one of Fine Arts? But I fancy we shan't ever have one, and that if we had one it would quake in abject terror of any vested interests.

And on that note of mild pessimism, Ladies and Gentlemen, I will bid you goodnight. I told you at the outset that my subject was an exciting one. If I haven't made it seem so to you, don't accuse me of breach of faith. I didn't promise you that *I* wasn't going to be rather dull. Besides, you must remember that not one of you has been listening to me for his or her own sake, for her or his own gratification. You have been listening All for Each, and Each for All.

PLAYGOING

[SUNDAY, 8 OCTOBER 1945]

LADIES AND GENTLEMEN, the title I have chosen for this soliloquy has rather an old-world flavour. But I myself am one of the relics of an older, an easier and more pleasant and yet a more formal world than this one, and my lips were loth to frame the modern equivalent, "Doing a Show." I might have said, "Going to the Play," which was a familiar phrase in the Victorian and Edvardian eras. Familiar but strange. The use of the definite article was so very indefinitive. Going to *what* play? There was always more than one; though certainly plays were fewer, and theatres fewer, and we had only two or three dramatists—only two or three, I mean, who were alive and also worth mentioning. In fact, for better or worse, things were very different. Let me maunder over some of the differences.

Actors and actresses were certainly regarded with far greater interest than they are nowadays. The outstanding ones inspired something deeper than interest. It was with excitement, with wonder and with reverence, with something akin even to hysteria, that they were gazed upon. Some of the younger of you listeners would, no doubt, if they could, interrupt me at this point by asking, "But surely you don't mean, do you, that our parents and grandparents were affected by them as we are by cinema stars?" I would assure you that those idols of ours were even more ardently worshipped than are yours. Yours, after all, are but images of idols, mere shadows of glory. Those others were their own selves, creatures of flesh and blood, there, before our eyes. They were performing in our presence. And of our presence they were aware. Even we, in all our humility, acted as stimulants to them. The magnetism diffused by them across the footlights was in some degree our own doing. You, on the other hand, have nothing to do with the performances of which you witness the result. Those performances—or rather those innumerable rehearsals—took place in some far-away gaunt studio in Hollywood or elsewhere, months ago. Those moving shadows will be making identically the same movements at the next performance, or rather at the next record; and in the inflexions of those voices enlarged and preserved for you there by machinery not one cadence will be altered. Thus the theatre has certain advantages over the cinema, and in virtue of them will continue to survive. But the thrill of it is not quite what it was in my young days.

In those piping days of yore, there was in playgoing a spice of adventure, of audacity. The theatre was frowned on by quite a large part of the community. The Nonconformist Churches were, without exception, dead against it. Ministers of even the Church of England were very dubious about it and never attended it. Players were no longer regarded in the eighteen-eighties and 'nineties as rogues and vagabonds, but the old Puritan prejudice against them still flourished. Not long ago I came across an excellent little book published in the 'sixties, entitled *A Manual for Chess Players*. It had as preface a very erudite history of the game, in the course of which occurred these words: "Chess has throughout the ages been the favourite pastime of all sorts and conditions of men, from Popes and Emperors to actors and dustmen." And here is another straw to show that the wind was still blowing briskly that way even in the 'eighties. A small boy, a son of that great actress, Mrs. Kendal, on his first day at a preparatory school in London, was asked by an elder boy, "Your mother's an actress, isn't she?" He replied with spirit, "If you say that again, I'll knock you down." I remember, too, that at the public school to which I was admitted in 1885 none of the boys, though my elder brother, Herbert Beerbohm Tree, was already a well-known actor, ever referred to our brotherhood. It was only in 1887, when Herbert became an actor-manager, that the silence was broken, that the subject ceased to be a delicate one. An actor-*manager* could be mentioned quite frankly, and even with awe.

Well, the days of the actor-manager are past. No doubt he was not a faultless institution. But he was an impressive and exciting one. There he was, in his own theatre, and giving to that theatre a definite individuality of its own. It was not merely a building, it was a kind of temple, with its own special brand of worshippers. First nights were thrilling, throbbing occasions. People had come not so much to see a mere play as to see a play with their idol in it. They hoped the play would be a success for *his* sake. If it seemed to them a failure, the pit and gallery booed the author for having betrayed their idol. They were in no mood to stand any nonsense from an author. Many of them had been sitting on camp-stools, or standing for hours and hours outside the theatre, patiently, smilingly, devotedly. Some of them even were quick to resent in one of the characters of the play any lack of right feeling for the leading man. I remember the first night of a play written for Mr. Lewis Waller—a play in which he was an important Anglo-Indian soldier, in a white uniform and in command of a province. In the second act there came to him an evil native with a petition of a kind that Mr. Waller could not grant. The native produced a pistol and fired it at him. I was in the back row of the stalls, and was almost deafened by a young lady who, in the front row of the pit, screamed "How *dare* he?"

I remember also a first night in which that excellent romantic actor, in his speech before the curtain, thanked the audience for their "loyalty" to him. And indeed that word was not inappropriate. Actor-managers were kings, in their fashion—in the English, the constitutional fashion: not autocrats in danger of their lives. In the daytime they drove about unguarded in hansom cabs—or even walked, taking the pavement with as easy a grace as that with which they took the boards.

They are gone. They have been replaced by theatrical syndicates. Are you thrilled when you see a syndicate sauntering down Piccadilly or driving down it in a *char-*

à-banc? Is your pulse quickened by the thought of the awful financial risks taken by these brave fellows? Do you pray that their box-offices will be for ever besieged? I fear you are coldly concerned with the mere question whether the play they are running is a good one, worthy of your respect. Even if they themselves were playing the male parts in it the sight of them out in the open air would not deeply stir you. The play, not so much the players nowadays, is what you are really keen on. "The play's the thing."

And it is, on the whole, a better thing than it used to be. In my very young days it was mostly something adapted from the French, and had suffered greatly in the Channel crossing. Henry Arthur Jones and Arthur Wing Pinero were almost alone in having both a sense of the theatre and a sense of the realities of life. And the Americans gave us no help. Mr. Augustin Daly's farces were then her sole export, and not at all a good one. America was very grateful for the imports she got from us. Meanwhile in Norway a great grim dramaturgist was every morning at his desk, unresting but unhurrying, giving to his compatriots one play every two years. And in England there was a Scotsman who knew the Norwegian tongue and translated the biennial achievement. Towards the end of the 'eighties he even managed to get the latest of those achievements produced precariously in some small theatre in London. The dramatic critics of that time were a less sophisticated race than the present one. They were a race of cheerful hacks. They did not see eye to eye with their argute Scottish colleague, William Archer, on the merits of *A Doll's House*. Even A. B. Walkley, though he of course recognised the magnitude of Ibsen, found Ibsen rather rebarbative; and Bernard Shaw, though promptly Ibsenite, had not yet become a dramatic critic. The Ibsen movement became more mobile later on, when a very dynamic and fervent little Dutchman, J. T. Grein, who was not at all content with being "something in the City" and being also Consul for Bolivia, rushed in, founded The Independent Theatre, and produced *Ghosts*. And lo, there was a terrific outcry against Ibsen. But there was also an earnest outcry *for* him, raised by people who had hitherto rather disdained the theatre. There was so much to be said for the Ibsen method—for the stage as just a three-walled room, with some people in it talking in a perfectly natural manner; not doing much, but thinking and feeling deeply; and illustrating some idea, and presenting some problem or other; and with no prospect of that happy ending to which the public was accustomed. And presently, under the Ibsen influence, Mr. Pinero wrote *The Second Mrs. Tanqueray*. I am told that it seems very artificial nowadays; but it seemed dreadfully, delightfully true to nature then. And anon came the Stage Society, with performances of earlier and later plays by Ibsen, and of plays by other more or less grim foreigners, and of a play or two already by Bernard Shaw. And very superior young men who had never thought of writing for the theatre began to do so, not without some measure of devious success. And in course of time it befell that Shaw became actually popular. Harley Granville-Barker, allied with Mr. Vedrenne, had brilliantly established himself in the Court Theatre, and it was there that *Man and Superman* was produced. Someone told King Edward that it was a play he ought to see. One night he came and saw it. Then came all rank and fashion to see it. And the bourgeoisie came to see *them*. And incidentally both the seers and the seen discovered that Shaw was really a most delightful person.

At that time I was a dramatic critic, and very angry that not all the theatres in London were given over to intellectual drama. I was still in that mood when, thirty-five years ago, I retired from dramatic criticism, and left London, and ceased to go to theatres. My nature then mellowed. I became tolerant of whatever might be going on behind my back. But I gathered from the newspapers that my former colleagues, especially the younger ones, seemed to grow more and more distressed about things, and I remember that in about 1912 I composed in my head a drinking-song for them. I didn't send it to them, for I was afraid they might think the metre too cheerful. It ran as follows:

In days of yore the Drama throve
Within our storm-bound coasts,
The Independent Theatre gave
   Performances of *Ghosts*.
Death and disease, disaster
   And downfall were our joy,
The fun flew fast and faster
While Ibsen was our Master
   And Grein was a bright Dutch boy, my boys,
   And Grein was a bright Dutch boy.

The Future of the Drama
   Was our theme day in, day out,
Pinero was most sanguine,
   Henry Arthur had no doubt.

"On, on!" cried William Archer,
  And no man was less coy
Than Shaw, that spring-heel'd marcher
  In *any* new deparcher,
    When Grein was a bright Dutch boy, my boys,
    When Grein was a bright Dutch boy.

The Movies moved not yet, my boys,
  Revues were not in view,
The present state of things was not
  Foreseen by me and you.
We sailed o'er seas uncharted
  Of youth and faith and joy.
None cried "Are we downhearted?"
In those dear days departed
    When Grein was a bright Dutch boy, my boys,
    When Grein was a bright Dutch boy.

For any man who has been and is no longer a dramatic critic there is a peculiar pleasure in playgoing, even if the play be a bad one, and even if the theatre be one of those austere, bleak, neutral-tinted, ferro-concrete tabernacles which the modern architect and his upholsterer seem to think preferable to such genial places as the Haymarket or the St. James's, and even if the players be seeming to forget that the room they are in is only a *three*-walled one, and that we are come to hear what they have to say. For such a man there is the bliss of knowing that he need not write one line about what is going on—need not be anxiously on the look-out for some point of view from which he could compose an article which readers would think clever and would enjoy. Oh yes, I assure you I am very mellow. If the bad old times, and with them the bad old tricks (the "soliloquy," the "aside," and so on) came in again, I think I should rather welcome them, for old sake's sake. And if intellectual ideas were to vanish from the boards I am not sure that my heart would break. Indeed, I have a sort of feeling that one can appreciate ideas, is more susceptible to them and better able to grapple with them, when they are set forth in a book that one is reading by one's own fireside than when they are mooted to an auditorium. One can pause, can linger, can perpend. I have a notion that the drama is, after all, essentially a vehicle for action (for drama, as the Greeks quite frankly called it), is essentially, or at least mainly, a thing to cause the excitement of pity and awe, or of terror, or of laughter, rather than to stimulate one's ratiocinative faculties. The theatre, I would say, is a place for thrills. You may, of course, be thrilled at your fireside by a book of philosophy or of history. You are still more likely to be so by a fine work of fiction. But the characters in a novel are not there before your very eyes, saying and doing things in your very presence. The novelist's power to startle you, or to hold you in breathless suspense, is a slight one in comparison with the dramatist's. All the vividest of my memories of the theatre are memories of stark "situations"—the appearance of the Ghost on the battlements at Elsinore; or the knocking at the gate while Duncan is murdered, and the repetition of that knocking; or the screen with Lady Teazle behind it, and the fall of that screen; or, in plays of later date, "Who are you?"— "HAWKSHAW, the detective!"—CURTAIN. Or "Disguise is useless! You are MACARI!" Or, in Oscar Wilde's classic farce, the appearance of John Worthing, in deepest mourning, at the garden gate, to announce the death of his figmentary brother.

Is this a Philistine standpoint? Well, I have no time to defend myself, and I fear you are glad that I haven't. I fear that you, Ladies and Gentlemen, have *not* been thrilled by *me* at your firesides, and are yearning for the next item on the programme: BARCAROLLE. And at this moment the Barcarollists are straining at the leash. Goodnight.

NAT GOODWIN—
AND ANOTHER

[MONDAY, 30 MAY 1949]

LADIES AND GENTLEMEN, from this year of grace it is a far cry to 1902, and perhaps you will not care to accompany me on so long a journey. But, at the risk of being my only listener, I say that in the autumn of that year my brother, Herbert Beerbohm Tree, occupied a house called Jackwood, on the top of Shooter's Hill. When I returned from my annual holiday in Dieppe to the duties of dramatic critic, he asked me to go there for the coming week-end. On the Saturday there was a "first night" at which I had to be present; so it was arranged that I should travel down, with a suitcase, after the performance. A cab was waiting for me when I arrived at Blackheath; and, while this vehicle climbed slowly, in the dead of night, the long steep hill up past Woolwich, I was filled with a vague sense of romance. To have been so lately in the glare of that theatre, and now to be here in these solitudes under the stars! Life seemed wonderful (though really, of course, it was I who was wonderful in being able to secure romance on such cheap terms). Had I been a conspirator in a strange land, finding my way towards some appointed spot for some fell purpose, I could not have been prouder of myself.

Perhaps the very fact that the land was *not* strange to me had something to do with my excitement. There is less romance in coming to a new place than in coming to one which you have known in other days. There is especial romance in coming to a house which you knew well before its present inmates were there—in seeing the old place under another dynasty. I had several times stayed in Jackwood when it was tenanted by Nat Goodwin, the American actor, and his wife, the beautiful Maxine Elliott. Always in the Spring, when the theatrical season "out there" was over, Nat Goodwin came to his "English home" (as he called it, with a deep fond drawl of the "o," making the English pronunciation of that word sound very trivial and heartless by comparison). On the stage he was one of the finest comedians I ever saw—the quietest and surest. Off the stage he had lived much in the company of prize-fighters, jockeys, professional card-players, and other folk whose good opinion was not a passport to the higher circles of life in the land of Emerson and Longfellow. But, as one often finds in the case of men who have lived wildly, he had preserved a flower-like simplicity of soul; and it was always a great joy to him to be at Jackwood, leading there what he believed to be the life of an English country-gentleman of the old school. He knew all about dogs and horses, loved them, had a wonderful way with them, and a fabulously expensive collection of them. One of the horses I remember especially: an enormous brown creature with a flashing eye, driven by Nat Goodwin in a fearsome little vehicle whose name I forget. It was a vehicle which Goodwin had brought over from America, and I think he regarded it as a rather false note in the English scene: he used to say, with a note of apology, that it was "vurry handy." It was appallingly handy. It consisted of nothing but two very large thin wheels with a sort of little basket slung low between for Goodwin and one friend to sit in. I was sometimes that one friend. The gigantic horse I regarded as our common enemy. There was nothing between him and the basket, and I think that had he dared he would have killed us both with a couple of well-directed kicks. But he dared not. He was a coward of cowards. There were few things he did not shy at, and from them he bolted. But who am I that I should sneer at him? He had at least the courage of his cowardice; not I of mine. I pretended to be enjoying those drives.

Travelling slowly now up that road which had been wont to flash past like lightning, I thought reverently of those old days—only two or three years old though they were. I reproached myself for coming to Jackwood under other auspices. Though I knew that Goodwin still owned the house, had tired of it, and was very glad to let it, I thought of him as the Old Squire expropriated—driven forth from the house of his forefathers, with a broken heart. There, where generations of simple, brave, God-fearing Goodwins had lived and died, the alien held high revel, the gross Beerbohm junketed. My heart was heavy when the cab passed through the old gates, which dated from the days of Queen Victoria. I was glad to see that the house was not brilliantly lit up within—glad when the servant who let me in said that the family had all gone to bed. I passed noiselessly into the dining-room, and there, under the influence of a cold partridge and a bottle of excellent Rhenish wine, gave rein to sentiment. Late the hour, but early in comparison with many hours I had spent in this room. The house had been designed and built for the late Lord Penzance—"Lord Penzance," Goodwin would say with unction, "President of your Court of Arches," but evidently not a smoker, for the house had no smoking-room. It was in the dining-room, therefore, that Goodwin cultivated, with rye whisky and ice and green cigars, the crescent hours of the morning. Blond and saturnine, he sat at the head of the table, very low down in his chair, staring at the smoke of his cigar, drawling interminable stories. Barring Charles Brookfield, he was the best actor of stories I ever heard; but these two men were of schools so different that it is absurd to compare them. Brookfield dealt in persons, Goodwin in types. Brookfield gave you the person, and the situation, and the point, in three quick flashes. Goodwin gave you the type, and the milieu, and the point if there was one, in a long sequence of minute and inimitable touches. The two men had but one excellence in common: utter lack of strain or effort. Brookfield shone hardly less as a commentator on life than as a portrayer of it. He was socially equipped at all points. Goodwin was a portrayer merely. As theorist he was primitive and bemused. It was true he could be witty. . . . He it was who said in a public speech, "They tell me I oughtn't to have gone in so much for Wine, Woman, and Song. Well, I'm going to give up singing." Once he was in a box in a New York Music Hall, to hear a "turn" in which a popular imitator gave an imitation of him. When this was over, the performer called out, "What d'yer think of it, Nat?" "One of us is damned bad," answered Goodwin. He was great in drollery.

But here in this dining-room he had not been great in the intervals between the stories of life out West or down South. Those intervals would grow longer as the night waned and the smoke thickened and the ice melted and the rye whisky ebbed in its decanter. Goodwin on Theology was not great; and it was to theology that he most tended in these intervals . . . "I once had a book called *Paley's Evidences*. Paley was a great Englishman, and you ought to be damned proud of him. . . . It's easy enough to be an Atheist, like Ingersoll. . . . Paley knew what he was talking about. Fine. . . . Paley convinced me. . . . I don't say every word in the Bible's true. No, sir. But the Sermon on the Mount—well, it's fine." In some such fashion Nat Goodwin would ramble on, emerging gradually from darkness into the light of another story, while daylight itself crept in through the windows to listen, and our laughter made inaudible the twittering of birds.

Where now were the echoes of that laughter? I wandered out from the silent room into the silent hall. It is always uncanny to be moving about in a house where you have not yet seen those others who sleep. Slightly shivering, I gazed around the familiar expanse of panelled hall, for some signs of habitation. And the first sign that caught my eye touched every nerve in me to astriction. Rigid, I stared at it across the hall. There it stood, upright and alone, on a long oaken chest that I remembered. Dim though the light was, I had no need to go nearer. I knew the thing. And I hasten to tell you, without keeping you in further suspense, that what I saw on that oaken chest, in that dim hall, was a hat. It was a silk hat, very tall, tapering somewhat from base to crown; and its brim was notably wide and flat. It was rather like the hats which Frenchmen wore in the Second Empire, and still more like the hats that were worn by the female peasants of Wales. But I was not misled into false hope by these casual resemblances. I knew the hat. I had often caricatured it—it and its wearer. I knew them both well by sight. I knew the wearer's works, too. I had written, in more than one of the public prints, very irreverently, very gallingly about some of those works. My caricatures of that worker, that wearer, they too had appeared in the public prints. With all the ribaldry of youth, I had persecuted Hall Caine. And here he was, under this roof. Here was his hat.

I stood as one frozen. Why had not my brother warned me? Nay, why had not I myself foreseen the dire likelihood? I had known that *The Eternal City* was in rehearsal at His Majesty's; and a manager and an author during the period of rehearsal are always more or less inseparable. . . . I looked at the front door. How easy to shoot back those bolts and flit! And yet I could not do it. Just that cowardice-within-cowardice which kept me exposed to that great wild horse of Nat Goodwin's held me now for exposure to this great wild author.

Next morning I awoke jaded with the sense of having dreamed awful things all through the night. In sleep,

where imagination is uncontrolled by reason, what flights
are taken by even the most unenterprising, the littlest and
least lurid minds! And it occurred to me to wonder, while
I bathed, "What must the dreams of a Hall Caine be
like?"

The act of shaving is a tonic. And Sunday morning and
a flood of September sunshine are sedatives. I reminded
myself that Hall Caine could not, in the phrase of the vulgar, eat me, and went downstairs holding my head high.

From the dining-room came a pretty sound of children
in song—a sound as of some little hymn being learned.
My vision, as I went in, included napery and cutlery, and
ham and eggs, and Hall Caine himself, and two little
nieces of mine, one on either side of their father's chair,
a paternal arm encircling each of them. The singing broke
off at the uncle's entry. There was a brotherly greeting,
an avuncular kiss was bestowed on two small cool brows,
Hall Caine's hand gripped mine, mine Hall Caine's.
"Now," said father to children, "try again, my darlings.
A *little* more together, this time. . . . Now!"

"Hail, hail, Hall Caine!
Thy glorious rays
Make bright our nights
And eke our days."

"There! That was much better," Herbert admitted.
"But not *quite* so good, my darlings, as it might be. Once
again!" Hall Caine flung back his head and hands, with a
glance at me and a facetious groan. I saw that he was
blushing—had been blushing before I came into the
room. And that very human blush endeared him to me

ever after. Mere fun though the hymn was, mere chaff, yet it was a sort of tribute, too. He liked it. It was a laughing tribute to fame. It was also and more directly a tribute to good-nature. "What a fellow it is!" his glance said to me of my brother; but his blush said more to me of himself. He may not have known that I knew—may not himself have known—just what his feelings were while those two little girls carolled. But he knew that somehow he and I were in sympathy. Something was established between us.

Of course, the past could not be undone. But gone was any resentment he may have had, and gone any little hostility that may have been in me. And it was not to relieve tension, but because the topic came pat, that he talked now to me, across the breakfast-table, of the sufferings caused to him by one of my drawings especially. This was a crude and unpretentious little design which I had almost forgotten. It showed Hall Caine, with frenzied eyes and hair, bearing a sandwich-board on which his name was inscribed in lavish capitals. It had been reproduced on a small scale in one of the English papers. But not there, I now learned from Hall Caine, was an end of it. He went to lecture in America, and, into whatsoever city he entered, always that presentment stared him in the face. It cropped up, with nerve-shattering iteration, in every local paper, often magnified to the scale of a full page. If it wasn't on the front page, there it was on the middle page. His impresario suggested that it might make a good poster. It pursued him, it wore him down. . . .

I said how sorry I was. I assured him that the drawing, in so far as I could remember it, was a failure. I pleaded that I had but seen him casually in theatres and other public places. Henceforth, having met him at close quarters, I should be able to do something more nearly like. A caricature done at sight was mere hit-or-miss—usually miss. At best it could only be superficial. True, one didn't have to know a man well before one could do a good caricature of him. On the contrary, as soon as one knew a man really well, one ceased to have a clear vision of him—took him rather as a matter of course. But acquaintance (said I, envisaging Hall Caine) was a necessity. A man's gestures, the movements of his face, the very tone of his voice—to say nothing of the tone of his mind—all these things the caricaturist needed to know before he could make a proper synthesis.

Yes, I used the word synthesis. I remember, because one of my little nieces asked the meaning of the word. I seldom used such words except in writing. But I was fluent enough in them when I spoke with authority; and, as caricature was one of the very few subjects about which I really did know something, "synthesis" said I. I tried to go even further. "Henceforth," I said to Hall Caine, "I shall be able to—to"—I wavered between synthesise and syntheticise—"to make a proper synthesis of you, you know."

I forget whether Hall Caine seemed as glad of this as I was. But—like to like—I think my earnestness pleased him. Certainly the caricatures I did of him in the future were much better than the old ones. I got the expression of his face, whereas previously I had got only the form. Familiar to me already was that great red river of hair which, from its tiny source on the mountainous brow, spread out so quickly and flowed down so strongly and gushed at last in such torrents over the coat-collar. Viewing these rapids from a practical standpoint, I had often thought it a pity that so much force should not be utilised somehow—for turning a mill-wheel, say, or working an electrical plant. But in the course of this Sunday at Jackwood I began to suspect that the great light of Hall Caine's eyes was indeed worked by this means; also the great and (so slight was his chest) astonishing resonance of his voice. His eyes, in their two deep caverns beneath the lower slopes of Mt. Brow, shone wondrously when he talked. His whole body seemed to quiver as though too frail for the powerful engines installed in it. I think it was this very frailty that gave to his talk, when he was in full swing, the peculiar effectiveness that it had. When a large, robust man talks loudly and well to you from the bottom of his soul, you are stirred, but not so much as when you are thus addressed by one whose body counts for so little that you seem to see as an almost physical thing the soul itself. The sight of an Atlantic liner in motion is grand; but you get a greater thrill from looking down through a hatch into the engine-room and seeing with your own eyes the monstrous forces of leaping and writhing steel there. Such a hatch—if I may say so without straining metaphor too far—was available on the surface of Hall Caine.

It was the fashion to decry him. I never, thank Heaven for self-respect! went to tea-parties. But I know that at tea-parties it was always possible to raise a titter by the mere mention of Hall Caine's name. More or less it was everywhere so. And there is no denying that Hall Caine had rather brought this on himself. There had come a time when he got himself interviewed too much, photographed too much, seen too much, advertised in every way too much. I think this lust for publicity may have been a result of residence with Dante Gabriel Rossetti.

Conceive: a raw and excitable stripling, caught suddenly from Liverpool into still more vital London, to live incessantly apart for almost two years with a man of genius who suffered from agoraphobia in an acute form. It was thought that Hall Caine lost too little time after Rossetti's death in bringing out a book about him. Poor young man!—I think it was natural that he should desire to lose not a moment. Light! air! publicity at any price and at once!—such was the quite inevitable and excusable reaction. Then followed years of steady, quiet work, of publication in the normal manner. "See," said the Muses to the Graces, "he has settled down. He will always be all right now." And Nature, overhearing them, smiled to herself grimly. All right—he? That one brief bout enough to counteract for ever all those long months at 16, Cheyne Walk? And, sure enough, suddenly one fine morning, out rushed Hall Caine into the market-place and chartered a cart and a trumpet and the biggest big drum that ever was made, and blew a blast on that trumpet, and in that cart, in that market-place, beating that drum with his left hand, wrote *The Christian*. Had he presently fled to the top of an ivory tower in the desert, and there hurled stones down at any one who dared come within a stone's throw, he could not have appeased the wrath of us superior persons. But he did not flee. He stayed where he was, abiding by his later manner. His popularity was enormous; but he had cheapened his work as well as his reputation. In his earlier work there was—there is—imagination, a strong dramatic sense, a very genuine humanity; not beauty; not restraint; but qualities enough for much admiration and gratitude. Nor from the later works were these qualities gone; but all smothered and bedevilled and annulled they were by the author's desire to spread himself out and be panoramic and a preacher and a prophet. Simple and strong dramatic crises of simple and strong human beings, with the Isle of Man for background—this was the prescription he ought to have stuck to and, but for Rossetti, would probably have stuck to. However, there is no use in repining. Greater joy was given to a greater number of people by Hall Caine's later than by his earlier manner. Let us others take comfort. I have already the special comfort I took, that morning at Jackwood, in the discovery that Hall Caine himself belonged to his earlier manner; human and direct, unassuming (though so very effective) and unspoiled.

After luncheon he was closeted with my brother; for he had come specially to discuss those various "cuts" and amplifications which in the course of a play's rehearsal often do seem desirable, even to the author. But, removed though he was from sight and hearing, I seemed to be aware of him all over the house. It was as though he sent out wide vibrations, like the screw of a vessel; and as the effect was to make me feel rather uncomfortable I was glad when, at tea-time, he reappeared in person. He showed signs of fatigue, and it is not unlikely that the confabulation had been rather a trial. My brother was always liked by any one who worked with him. He was intuitive, easy, eager, and generous-minded. But his sense of humour was not under control; and I think Hall Caine had often a difficult time with him. "A little tomfoolery in our hours of relaxation is most wholesome"—I can imagine that sentiment cherished by Hall Caine. But my brother was apt to gambol at the most inauspicious moments; and the very sublimity of Hall Caine's earnestness was a standing temptation. I think there may have been some such gambols on this Sunday afternoon at Jackwood. But after a cup of tea Hall Caine was himself again and talking as well as ever. He complained that in one respect the critics were hardly just to him. I noticed that he did not call them the critics, but the Gentlemen of the Press. This phrase, usual and null though it is at a Public Dinner, seemed to take on an extraordinary significance, an awe-inspiring "value," in private life. There mysteriously it implied at once a compliment and an indictment. I was dramatic critic of *The Saturday Review*. It was borne in on me that *I* was a Gentleman of the Press. I had never thought of myself in that light—or was it that darkness? It was both; and I experienced pride and shame. "The Gentlemen of the Press," I heard Hall Caine saying, "twit me with being melodramatic." His argument was that if what they deemed to be melodrama was melodrama and nothing else, then all the serious dramatists since the world began had abounded in melodrama. He gave examples. I saw that if We Gentlemen of the Press were right in our first principles, then was Shakespeare essentially a melodramatist. My new-found *esprit de corps* forbade me to abandon those principles, and I knew that Shakespeare wasn't melodramatic, but—well, what *were* our first principles exactly? I never had any presence of mind in argument. With men of my own age, I usually lost my temper—I, who so depended on being always suave. Among my elders, a very real modesty saved me from such loss by debarring me from conflict—even if these elders happened to be so old as to be no more than a match for me. Had Hall Caine been as old as Methuselah I would not have interrupted him. The fact that he wasn't yet fifty set an additional seal on silence. Besides, I liked listening to him.

It is dangerous doctrine, for mankind at large, that first impressions are always right. They are certainly the sharpest, and therefore the hardest to erase, and their resistant quality is often mistaken for righteousness in them. But they are trustworthy enough in people who have an intuition for character. People who have that gift are not indeed to congratulate themselves that it is a great one. There are other gifts which I should much prefer to have had—intellect, imagination, bravery, moral fervour, and so on. But, such as it is, I am grateful for this gift. It saves me no end of trouble. If my first impressions happen to be wrong, they are erased with comparative ease because my mind is of so susceptible a substance. And the fact is that they very seldom are wrong. Wrong, I mean, *for me*. I am not such a fool as to pretend to see any object "as in itself it is." No man can do that. Or rather, no man can know that he has done that. I claim but the power to see rather quickly Mr. This or Mr. That as he appears to me and as he probably would still appear to me if I spent the rest of my life with him on a desert island. Fate decreed that Hall Caine and I should not live together on a desert island. Fate went so far as to decree that I should not often meet him after that first time. But those few other meetings—they and some letters I had from him on a matter that concerned us both—strengthened my first impressions of him. And I think of him always not only as a man of great force and magnetism, but as one who had a rare sweetness and sincerity of character, and was very simple and kind and good.

(WRITTEN 1912)

GEORGE MOORE

[FRIDAY, 6 OCTOBER 1950]

WHEN, WHERE, did I first see my friend George
Moore? It is odd that I do not remember my first
sight of him. For I am sure there never was in heaven or
on earth any one at all like him. It is conceivable that in
the waters that are under the earth there *may*, vaguely
luminous, be similar forms, and—stay, it isn't odd, after
all, this lapse of my memory. It is explained by that quality of luminous vagueness which Moore's presence always
had. There always was an illusory look about him—the
diaphanous, vaporous, wan look of an illusion conjured
up for us, perhaps by means of mirrors and by a dishon-
ourable spiritualist. There was something blurred about
him; his outlines seemed to merge into the air around him.
He never seemed to enter or leave a room. Rather did he
appear there, and in due time fade thence. It was always

difficult to say at what moment he appeared: one had but become aware of his presence, which was always delightful, and later one found oneself missing him: he had gone. Thus would it be a strange feat indeed if now I remembered more than this: that somewhere in the early 'nineties the apparition of Moore had already been vouchsafed me.

Mentally, as well as physically, he was unique. He was always the same, and yet always new. Perhaps his novelty was in part due to his sameness. The outer and inner demeanour of almost every man is variable, changing with the circumstances he is in and the sort of people who are about him. Except Oscar Wilde, I never knew a man whose tone of mind and mode of expression, everywhere and with everyone, were so invariable as Moore's. And whereas Oscar Wilde's personality was in great measure a conscious and elaborate piece of work, and outshone other personalities by reason of the finer skill that had gone to the making of it, as well as to the richer materials from which it was made, Moore's slighter but not less peculiar personality was an entirely natural product. That he was intensely self-conscious is proved in all his many autobiographies. On the other hand, it is clear in his writings, and was still more clear to me in personal acquaintance with him, that he never exercised any positive guidance of himself. He was content to look on at himself, sometimes rather admiringly, more often disparagingly, always with absolute detachment. While he swam he looked on from the bank, and never when he sank did he offer himself a helping hand. For well or ill, he just let himself be; and as the spectacle of himself was too interesting to be interfered with even for his own sake, of course he wouldn't interfere with it to please Brown, Jones, and Robinson. It was for this reason that he was so dear to Wilson Steer, Tonks, and Walter Sickert, and indeed to all people who had the wit to enjoy in the midst of an artificial civilisation the spectacle of one absolutely natural man.

Whatever was in his mind, no matter where he was nor what his audience, he said. And when he had nothing to say, he said nothing. Which of these courses in an average drawing-room needs the greater courage—to say simply anything, or to sit saying simply nothing? I think I used to rate Moore's silences his finer triumph. They were so unutterably blank. And yet, in some remote way, they so dominated the current chatter. It was impossible not to watch him during them. He sat rather on the edge of his chair, his knees together, his hands hanging limp on either side of him. Limply there hung over his brow a copious wisp of blond hair, which wavered as he turned the long white oval of his face from one speaker to another. He sat wide-eyed, gaping, listening—no, one would not have said "listening" but hearing: it did not seem that his ears were sending in any reports to his brain. It would be an understatement to say that his face was as a mask which revealed nothing. His face was as a mask of gauze through which Nothing was quite clearly visible. And then, all of a sudden, there would appear—Something. There came a gleam from within the pale-blue eyes, and a sort of ripple passed up over the modelling of the flaccid cheeks; the chin suddenly receded a little further, and—*Voilà Moore qui parle! Silence, la compagnie! Moore parle.*

What Moore spoke of would be always something quite alien to the general theme. It would be some i-de-a that had lately been simmering in his brain. He had come to the conclusion that the eighteenth century was a *stoopid* century; or he had been reading Milton, and saw now that Shelley was not a poet after all; or he saw now that women had no e-motion, but only logic. . . . Always an i-de-a, delivered hot and strong, in gulps, as from the spout of a kettle boiling over. He had (as I have typographically suggested here) a way of dividing the syllables of his words, and of giving to each syllable an equal stress. Such words as *the* and *a* and *of* and *to* he pronounced as emphatically as any other word; and the effect was that they seemed to have an emphasis beyond all others; it was as though his voice *bulged* when he came to them. I suppose this habit of equal stress was due to his having lived among Frenchmen and talked French during his most malleable years. His Parisianism, grafted upon an imperishable brogue, gave to his utterance a very curious charm. Aided by his face and his gesture, this charm was irresistible. I say his "gesture" advisedly; for he had but one. The finger-tips of his vague, small, inert, white hand continually approached his mouth and, rising thence, described an arc in the air—a sort of invisible suspension-bridge for the passage of his i-de-a to us. His face, too, while he talked, had but one expression—a faintly illumined blank. Usually, when even the most phlegmatic of men is talking, you shall detect changes of expression. In Moore you never could. Usually the features of the most vivacious man's face retain the form that Nature assigned to them. But in Moore's face, immutable though the expression was, by some physical miracle the features were perpetually remoulding themselves. It was not merely that the chin receded and progressed, nor

merely that the oval cheeks went rippling in capricious
hollows and knolls: the contours of nose and brow, they
too, had their vicissitudes. You think I exaggerate? Well,
I myself, with Moore there before me, did sometimes
doubt the evidence of my own eyes. It was possible that
my eyes had been deceived. But the point then is that no
face save Moore's ever deceived them in just this way.

Sometimes he talked, as sometimes he also wrote in
books, about ladies who had loved him. On such occasions, either because I had never met any of these ladies,
or because the conventional English education instils into
us a prejudice against that kind of disquisition, I used not
to listen very attentively—used to revel merely in the visual aspect of this man of genius. Genius, assuredly, he
had; not, I think, in his specifically creative work; but in
criticism, yes. His novels, always interesting though they
were, never seemed to me to have the quality of life. I
saw them rather as experiments, made with admirable
skill and patience and, as the years passed, on an ever-
increasing scale—experiments which, though all the
proper materials had been collected, and all the latest sci-
entific formulae mastered, somehow failed of that final result for which they were made: creation of authentic life.
Moore's habit of rewriting his earlier novels was in itself
the deadliest criticism they could have. When once a novel
has left the writer's hand, and been published, the characters, if they really live, are beyond his power. What they
were, what they did, what happened to them, are things
as unalterable now as the character and career of the late
Queen Victoria. If they do not unalterably live for the
man who made them, for whom shall they live? And if
they do not live, how shall belated life be breathed into

the clay? Vital magic, which was just what his novels lacked, was just what his criticisms had. No one but Ruskin has written more vividly than he, more lovingly and seeingly, about the art of painting; and no one has ever written more inspiringly than he, with a more infectious enthusiasm, about those writers whom he understood and loved, or more amusingly against those whom he neither understood nor liked. Of learning he had no equipment at all; for him everything was a discovery; and it was natural that Oscar Wilde should complain, as he did once complain to me, "George Moore is always conducting his education in public." Also, he had no sense of proportion. But this defect was, in truth, a quality. Whenever he discovered some new old master, that master seemed to him greater than any other: he would hear of no other. And it was just this frantic exclusiveness that made his adorations so fruitful: it was by the completeness of his surrender to one thing at a time that he possessed himself of that thing's very essence. The finest criticism is always passive, not active. Mastery comes only by self-surrender. The critic who justly admires all kinds of things simultaneously cannot love any one of them, any more than a lady can be simultaneously in love with more than one gentleman. That kind of critic is often (if I, who am of that kind, may be allowed to say so) very admirable. But it is the Moores who matter.

When I say that Moore could revere only one master at a time, I do not mean that he was always faithless to old idols. When he had exhausted his ecstasy at some new shrine, he would rise from his knees and, if no other new shrine were visible, would wander back to some old one. Turgéneff, especially, had power to recapture and reinflame him ever. Almost the last time I met him was in one of these recurrent intervals. We were both of us, for the week-end, guests of Mr. Hugh Hammersley and his brilliant and beautiful wife. On Saturday evening, and on Sunday, Moore was rather blank. We could not tempt him to talk. I saw that he had risen from before some shrine, and was temporarily at a loss. At dinner on Sunday I mentioned Turgéneff. It was as though I had taken him by the hand, poor waif, and led him to the place where he would be. It was as though he leapt across the familiar threshold of the temple and fell prostrate at the shrine. At bed-time he was still talking of Turgéneff with unflagging charm and power. And when, next morning, rather late, I came down to breakfast, there, fresh as a lily that had bloomed in the night—there at the breakfast-table, with a fork in his right hand while his left described innumerable arcs over a plate of haddock—was Moore, talking of Turgéneff to our polite host.

It is a pity for mankind that Moore's eloquence was all chamber-music. When I said just now that he was always the same "everywhere" I meant that he was always the same among his diverse friends and acquaintances. In public he simply evaporated. In his *Ave* he has called himself "the only Irishman who could not make a speech"; and to this testimony I can add that he could not passably read a speech. I was a guest at that public dinner of which in *Ave* he has given an immortal account—the dinner held at the Shelbourne Hotel, Dublin, to inaugurate the Irish Literary Theatre; and well do I remember the woebegone way he murmured into his MS., making in that convivial and pugnacious company of orators no effect whatsoever. Nor was this the first time I had seen him wilt in the publicity he abhorred. In '96 Mr. Joseph Pennell sued *The Saturday Review* and "Another" for libel. "Another" was Walter Sickert, who had written the offending criticism. The case hinged on the difference between lithographs drawn on paper and lithographs drawn directly on the stone. Whistler, who was no longer on speaking terms with Sickert, nor on speaking terms with very many people beside Mr. and Mrs. Pennell, threw his mantle over the plaintiff. The friends of Sickert combined to throw their own modest little mantles over "Another." Moore was always accounted a rather selfish man; but the fact that he, with his horror of public appearances, did volunteer for service in the witness-box is proof that he could on occasion barter self for Auld Lang Syne. . . . I can see him now, penned there, more than ever wraith-like in the harsh, bleak light of the court. He kisses the book, he acknowledges that his name is George Moore, and that he is an art critic; and dimly he conveys an impression that he prefers lithographs drawn directly on the stone. Up rises the cross-examining counsel: "Now, Mr. Moore, I want you to explain what claim you have to be regarded as an expert in this matter." Silence reigned. Moore's gaze wandered to the judge, and then suddenly his tongue was loosened. "I know Degas," he began; whereat down sat the cross-examining counsel with an eloquent gesture to judge and jury; the judge made a little gesture to the witness; the ordeal was over. But, brief though that ordeal was, I hope it will not go unrecorded in the Golden Book of Friendship and Self-Sacrifice.

Sickert, Steer, Tonks—these, I think, were the friends he valued most. They were more or less coeval with him, and they were painters. It was with painters that he was happiest. To them he could talk, with the certainty that they would sympathise, about painting, and about literature without being interrupted. They, on their side, revered him as the one mere critic with whom they could talk as with one of themselves. His face, too—that face transferred to canvas by so many painters since Manet—always entranced them with those problems of "planes" and "values" in which it abounded. He was always a sort of special *treat* to them. They went to him as children to a pantomime. Even more than his felicities of thought did they love those sudden infelicities which he alone could have uttered—those *gaffes* hailed with roars of delight that grew in volume while Moore stared around in simple wonderment. . . . "I have been told," he said suddenly, one evening, "that Mi-chael An-ge-lo carved the Da-vid from a block of marble that had been im-properly quarried. Now if any one gave me a block of marble that had been im-properly quarried, I could no more carve the Da-vid than—than I could fly!" And then "What is the joke? Tell me the joke. If there is a joke, and let me share it with you. If it is a good joke," etc., etc.

We know that the Irishman in England is not always what he seems. Moore, deep down in his breast, may have consciously cultivated and developed that innate quaintness which so pleased his friends. If he did so, this was his one little deviation from stark nature, and shall be forgiven him. But I don't really think he did so. Among people who refused ever to take him seriously, and were bent merely on teasing him, he would have dropped the pretence. One of these people—their ringleader, I might say—was Edmund Gosse, who loved to entertain Moore at his table, for the sake of the lavish en-

tertainment he found in Moore. He had, it is true, a great
admiration for Moore's endless patience in the craft of
literature; but in social intercourse Moore was but the
dearest, the least spared of all his butts. He drew Moore
out, he goaded him, he danced around him, he lightly
flew at him as a banderillero flies lightly at a bull, dexter-
ously planting ornamental darts adown either flank of
him. Moore never charged. He gazed mildly at his tor-
mentor, and patiently chewed the cud. He thought "Gosse
is very wit-ty. I wish I were so wit-ty as Gosse," and was
not at all deflected from his usual manner. . . . "I have
been reading," he would say, "a most as-tounding book."

G O S S E [*with a little start and a cry*]: Ah, I always forget that you can read—always I think of you as just a
writer. But you learnt to read when you were a child: I remember you once told me so, yes. And so you've been
reading a book? Now [*beaming a quick side-long glance
to the company*] tell us what that book was.

M O O R E [*diverting an absolutely blank gaze from host
to company*]: I have been reading *Don Quixote*.

G O S S E [*dartingly*]: In the original Spanish, no doubt?

M O O R E [*blankly envisaging him*]: No, in a translation. For of Spanish I know not one word. But now that I
have read *Don Quixote* I am very sorry that I do not know
Spanish, and that it is too late for me to learn Spanish.

G O S S E : Too late? Shame on such phrases! We'll go
to learn Spanish together, you and I, hand in hand, every
evening, to one of those night-schools.

M O O R E [*to the company*]: Ah, now Gosse is laughing at me, because Gosse is wit-ty, and if a man is as wit-ty
as Gosse, then he must have always somebody to laugh at.

G O S S E : Eliminate me, Moore! Or rather, regard me

as the gravest and most receptive of my sex. And so you have been reading *Don Quixote* in a translation? Dear, dear! Dr. Douglas Hyde's translation into Erse?

M O O R E [*his jaw dropping, and a sudden dawn of intense amusement visible in his eyes*]: Hyde has translated *Don Quixote* into Erse?

G O S S E : I've not the slightest doubt that he has. Ah [*lyrically*], what has he *not* done? What vistas of enchantment has he *not* opened up to the peasants who sit weeping around the waters of Shoo-na-Groo, and the peasants who go dreaming on the hills of Brau-na-Thingumy? Ah, if only poor dear Cervantes could know what delight— but there! You were just going to tell us all about him. Now we want to know just how he struck you.

M O O R E : The most a-mazing thing a-bout the book is—

G O S S E : That Sancho Panza is obviously mad from the outset?

M O O R E : I had not thought of that. [*Thinks of it, with growing pleasure in the idea.*] That is a good i-de-a, Gosse. I do not say that it is a true i-de-a. But an i-de-a is an i-de-a whether it be . . . [*His voice drifts into silence, then suddenly bursts forth.*] Why did not Cervantes treat Dulcin-e-a sub-jec-tive-ly? What manner of woman was she? Don Quixote speaks of her as his mistress. That is not e-nough. One wants to know . . . etc., etc.

The foregoing dialogue is of course apocryphal. (My memory, retentive though it is, isn't so retentive as all that.) But it suggests, with no tinge of exaggeration that I can see in reading it, Gosse's way with Moore, Moore's with Gosse. . . . Only, I haven't yet in these pages about Moore exemplified the goodness of his talk. I have merely

said how good it was, and given examples of its queer-
ness. . . . Oh, he too was often wit-ty. His mind, slow
though it was in opposition, could leap swift and far on
clear ground. Once, when the painting of "still life" was
being discussed, he thus routed the conversation: "I don't
care twopence about still life. Of what interest to me is it
to see a picture of a bunch of grapes, a—a postage stamp
and a pair of corduroy trousers?" How perfectly delicious
a generalisation! Of a certain very handsome and statu-
esque actress, whose performances were much admired
in the 'seventies, he said "I never could bear her. She was
like *most* of the policemen, and *all* the barmaids, in London."

It was odd that whenever he dropped such crystals as
these, he seemed to be as surprised by his friends' laughter as he was after one of his *gaffes*. Wit-ty, he was yet no
judge of wit; and he would sometimes appropriate and repeat without acknowledgement very inferior remarks
made by other people. I had a personal experience of this
foible. On the Sunday evening before he went to Dublin
for the inauguration of Irish drama, he and I had met at
the Gosses'. He had been inveighing against Kipling; and,
as we walked away together along Delamere Terrace, I
said that I thought Kipling fifty years hence would be remembered no more nor less than Martin Tupper was remembered now. Moore paused under a lamp-post. "That
is a-mazingly good," he exclaimed. "Fifty years hence
Kipling will be remembered only as Martin Tupper is remembered today! Oh but you really must let me say that
in my speech!" Next morning he went to Dublin. I went
next night. On Tuesday I was present at a luncheon which
he has described in *Ave*—a luncheon given by Mr. T. P.

Gill. I sat exactly opposite to Moore. Either Yeats or Mr. Gill mentioned the name of Kipling. "Oh," said Moore, "Kipling! Fifty years hence Kipling will be remembered only as Martin Tupper is remembered today!" We all laughed our appreciation, and I especially murmured "Capital!" Dear Moore had entirely forgotten me as maker of his remark, such as it was. He didn't make it in his actual speech on the following Thursday. I suppose he had made a rule never to repeat himself.

It was said that in his books, too, he sometimes incorporated as his own the sayings of other people. When *Evelyn Innes* appeared, my friend Clyde Fitch, the brilliant American dramatist, an annual visitor to London, was startled at finding that the description of Evelyn's acting of Marguerite in Gounod's *Faust* was already familiar to him. A year or so before, he had written in an English weekly paper, *The Musician,* a detailed appreciation of Madame Calvé's interpretation of the part at Covent Garden Opera House. The article was one of about a thousand words. Almost all of these, with a very slight emendation here and there, had been appropriated by Moore. I asked Clyde Fitch what he was going to do about it. But Clyde Fitch was a very good-humoured fellow, and said he wasn't going to do anything at all about it.

Perhaps it was apropos of this touching little theft in broad daylight that I said a rather good thing which, as I have not in my time said many good things, you must let me quote to you. D. S. MacColl and I and dear old William Nettleship, the painter, who was one of the most fervent delighters in Moore, were talking of realism in fiction. "I'm afraid," said Nettleship, "Moore's sometimes rather heavy-handed." "Perhaps; but he's awfully light-fingered," said I. . . . Now that I have made this quotation of myself, the excuse I gave for it seems not good enough. I am sure Moore wouldn't have thought it worth borrowing.

Often, when I met some perfect type of average English gentleman, I used to wonder in what degree he would have been more exciting, more of an individual, had he not gone to a Public School and a University. In presence of a true eccentric, conversely, I would wonder how much of him this curriculum, had he been cast into it, might have marred. For academic debate within my breast no question was more fascinating than this: How far would Moore have been less Mooreish if, in those malleable years of his, he had gone (say) to Eton and Oxford, instead of to Ballyhooly and Paris? It wouldn't really (I like to think) have made much difference. Oxford might in her own way have tinged, as Paris in hers tinged, his brogue. And he might have gone through life thinking his soul rather Oxfordish, even as he did go on thinking it rather Parisian. In his nonage, perhaps, Moore's soul did have a veneer of Paris; but this, thin and friable, was all gone before I knew him. . . . A few years ago, a friend of mine, who knew him only by sight and repute, saw him one day in Paris. By collocation of dates, I think this must have been at the time when Moore, as he told us in *Ave,* had crossed the Channel in order that he might write in French that Irish play which was to be translated into English by Lady Gregory, and thence into Erse by Mr. O'Donaghue, and thence back into English by Lady Gregory for final and magical treatment by Yeats. My friend, who would have supposed from repute that in Paris on a fine afternoon Moore would either be making love to

Mme. la Comtesse de Quelquechose in the Faubourg St.
Germain or be bandying heterodoxies in a conclave of
poets outside some little café on the Rive Gauche, was
surprised to see him in the Reading Room of the Grand
Hôtel, poring over *The Illustrated London News* and
presently hovering impatiently near the arm-chair of an
old gentleman who for too long a time had been monopo-
lising *The Graphic*.

In Paris he might have seemed to belong more or less
to London; but not so in London. Wherever a true individuality may be found, there recognisably is *not* its home.
Sometimes I used to see Moore dining in the Café Royal,
on the ground-floor—a haunt of which you could say that
it was neither French nor English; neutral territory (like
that Reading Room overseas); no-man's-land. Here
seemed to be, not indeed a home for him, but a fairly
congruous background. He himself, I think, knew that the
other scenes of London looked rather odd in relation to
him. "If you did not know me—if you just saw me in the
street," he said once to Sickert, "what should you guess
me to be?" The question demanded thought. "Should you
not," he pursued, with a touch of impatience, "guess me
to be an English country-gentleman, who had come up to
London to see his lawyer?" And then "What is the joke?
Tell me the joke. If there is a joke," etc., etc. . . . No,
assuredly, no passer-by would have attributed Moore to
our simple English countryside. He could ride a horse
well, I was told, and was quite a good shot, "but hang it!"
Sir William Eden once said to me, "he always comes
down to breakfast in pumps." And this reminds me that
it was in shooting over the coverts at Windlestone that he
met with an accident of which the sequel (as related by

him to Sickert and myself) illustrated most exquisitely his indifference to the codes of behaviour that govern us timid creatures of convention. A young man who was staying in the house and was one of the shooting-party fired off his gun at some wrong moment, and in some wrong direction; and the result was that a spent shot, glancing off a tree, badly grazed the surface of one of Moore's eyes. The sufferer was hurried back to the house, and surgically treated, and had to lie for some days in his darkened bedroom. On the second day, the guilty youth came to the bedside, to express his contrition. "And what," we asked Moore, as he described the scene to us in London, "what did you say?" "I said 'Oh, go a-way. I do not want ever to see you. You are an id-i-ot. For heaven's sake, go a-way,' and I turned on my pillow." How much better, after all, because how much more sincere, this was than the prescribed "My dear fellow, it's nothing! Don't say another word! Sort o' thing might happen to any one!" Such phrases as these would not have implied any true forgiveness; whereas Moore, having uttered his mind, was free to bear no ill-will. The tone in which he spoke to us of the young man was perfectly good-humoured. It might, of course, have been less so if the accident had been more serious. Luckily, no lasting damage had been done. "In fact," said Moore, unconsciously taking for a moment the famous posture of the Widow Wadman, "the eye is rather a pret-ti-er colour."

The thought that passed through the mind of Julia Hazeltine, when she found the Maestro Jimson hiding under the table in the deserted house-boat—"Surely this is very strange behaviour. He cannot be a man of the world!" —was precisely the thought raised by Moore in the minds of all worldly persons who met him for the first, or indeed the hundred-and-first, time. Yet neither would the unworldly have dreamed of claiming him for themselves. He shocked them. He was as one dangling to them the lures of levity and life. Of Edward Martyn, sitting stout in his tower at Tillyra, alone, cultivating his soul among his tomes of theology, Moore gave us in *Ave* a wonderful study—a study whose ridicule could not have been one tithe so good had it not been based on sympathy and affection. And Martyn, I believe, reciprocated fully these feelings. He liked to learn from Moore about modern painting, in return for what he taught him about old music. But certain it is that he was also afraid of Moore, afraid of his influence; and once, I am told, he gave to his fear deathless expression in a simple phrase, pensively uttered while he knocked the ashes from his pipe: "Well, he's a bhit of a bhank-holiday fellow, ye know, Moore is."

A marvellous phrase, that; an absolutely perfect rendering of the emotion behind it; but as a full judgment, of course, it cannot be accepted, nor have been intended. A man must be judged by what is fine in him, not by what is trivial; for the fine qualities must have deep roots within him, whereas trivial ones may thrive from the very surface. The bhank-holiday side of Moore, if there it was, can count for nothing as against the fine things inside him —his matchless honesty of mind; his very real modesty about his own work; his utter freedom from jealousy; his loving reverence of all that in all arts was nobly done; and, above all, that inexhaustible patience of his, and courage, whereby he made the very most of the gifts he had, and earned for himself a gift which Nature had not bestowed on him: the specific gift of *writing*. No young man—nay, no young woman—ever wrote worse than young Moore wrote. It must have seemed to every one that here was a writer who, however interesting he in himself might be, never would learn to express himself tolerably. Half a crown, we know, may be the foundation of a vast fortune. But what can be done without a penny? Some of the good writers have begun with a scant gift for writing. But which of them with no gift at all? Moore is the only instance I ever heard of. Somehow, in the course of long years, he learned to express himself beautifully. I call that great.

(WRITTEN 1913)

MARIE LLOYD

[MONDAY, 8 JANUARY 1951]

YOU MUST FORGIVE ME, Ladies and Gentlemen, for
being rather at a loss. Douglas Cleverdon wishes that
I should wind up this programme with a few words; and
here I am, in Italy, on January the third, winding it up
without having heard one word of it: not one word of it
has yet been recorded. In my young days I didn't only go
to Music Halls: I used to go also to the House of Commons, to hear Mr. Asquith winding up a debate on behalf
of the Opposition, and Mr. Balfour on behalf of the Government; or vice versa. They were lucky: they had heard
the debate. I can but humbly imagine what Compton
Mackenzie and Colin McInnes will have been saying
about Marie Lloyd. Of course they won't have debated
her: they will have agreed as to the magnitude of that lit-

tle person, and the magic of her, and you will have agreed with them.

I wonder which of her songs you like best. "Oh, Mr. Porter" was always my favourite—the flurry, the frantic distress of it: "I wanted to go to Birming*ham* and they're taking me on to Crewe." The accent was always on the last syllable of Birmingham; which helped the rhythm. Rhythm was one of her strong points. She had an exquisitely sensitive ear, impeccable phrasing and timing. But sheer joy of living was always her strongest point of all. Even in the agony of being taken on to Crewe, Mahrie— for that was how we pronounced her name—was bursting with rapture, and made us partakers of it.

And even in her last days, when her health failed and her movements were slow and heavy, and her song "I'm a thing of the past, old dear," she had not lost her spirit: she could mock her own infirmities. I wonder whether she foresaw the permanence of her fame. It is strange that of all the women of the Victorian Era the three most generally remembered are Queen Victoria herself, and Miss Florence Nightingale, and—Mahrie.

SIR DESMOND MacCARTHY

[SUNDAY, 22 JUNE 1952]

I FEEL SURE that most of you will at one time and another have heard the voice of Desmond MacCarthy
on the air, and, having heard it, will remember the charm
of it—the endearing intimacy of it. It was essentially
chamber music. One rather wondered that anything so
gentle could be carrying so far and wide. I always felt that
Desmond was in the room with me, with me and one or
two listeners only. But if he had been, the chances were
that he would have interrupted himself in his dulcet flow
by bringing one into the conversation. Eager talker though
he was, he was an equally keen listener, a great educer of
talk from other people. He would sit leaning far forward,
a picture of receptivity, very often murmuring pensively
"I see—I see." He was also a great user of that attractive,
that beguiling phrase "And tell me." This habit of his

(101)

may have been due partly to the Irish wish to please. But mainly, I think, it came of sheer modesty, sheer good fellowship. All but a few of the best talkers I have heard were Irishmen; and of them all Desmond, I think, was the one who, because he was more interested in other people than in himself, gave the greatest pleasure and was the most sought after by the greatest number of householders. He was one of the leading lights in the salon of Virginia and Leonard Woolf, and I remember being told by her of a stratagem that had been practised in order that for once Desmond's talk should not be unpreserved, be unrecorded. On a certain evening, behind a tall screen in the drawing-room, a professional stenographer was installed. This was beknown to all the frequenters of the salon, except of course Desmond. And Desmond was in his very best form. But, Virginia Woolf admitted, the typescript was a disappointment. Without the inflections of the voice, without the accompanying gestures and changes of facial expression, how could it have been otherwise? Readers of memoirs and diaries of social life in London of the early years of the nineteenth century will have come across many an account of Tom Moore at the piano, after this or that dinner-party, singing his Irish ballads, and causing thrills of emotion among all the ladies and gentlemen. Of course a gramophone record of his performance would not have had that effect. Tom Moore himself had to be there, with his own magnetism. Desmond too was magnetic, as are all good talkers. Certain rays forthcome from them.

Talk was Desmond's natural medium for expression. In writing he never acquired self-confidence and facility. Writing was always to him a task and rather a terror. And that is perhaps the reason why he wrote so splendidly well.

He had always to do his very best. Sometimes I regretted that he had been destined to write mostly about books; for I have always been less greatly interested in books than in human beings: I had not one whit of Desmond's scholarship; whereas Desmond's instinct for human life and character was impassioned and unerring, and I delighted most of all in his portrayals of men known to him —such as Samuel Butler, for example, and Mr. Asquith, and Henry James. How vividly they live in the pages he devoted to them! As vividly as he himself abides, and will abide always, in my memory, talking as only he could, and trying, from time to time, to efface himself with the words "And tell me," and "I see, I see." . . .

FIRST MEETINGS WITH
W. B. YEATS

[SUNDAY, 26 DECEMBER 1954]

LADIES AND GENTLEMEN, almost forty years ago I wrote, but didn't publish, a few little essays about meetings with interesting contemporaries of mine. One of these was about my first meetings with W. B. Yeats.

Before reading this little piece to you, I must explain that at that time Yeats had not begun to develop his great gifts in the manner in which he ultimately did. Of the fullness and richness of his later self there was as yet, for me, no token.

At Charterhouse, one morning, a small boy construed thus a rather difficult line of Euripides: "And a tear shall lead the blind man." "H'm," said his form-master, "clever tear!" Thereat we all laughed. But ought we to have

laughed? Granted, the translation was hopelessly inaccu-
rate. But in itself was not the image beautiful, and expressed in terms simple and sensuous, if not passionate?
I am led to ask this because, in after years, when first I
read some of the poems of W. B. Yeats, those words came
back to my memory, and seemed to have been inspired by
his own Muse. "And a tear shall lead the blind man" . . .
how easily, how well (thought I, and still think), might
some poem of this distinguished and true poet end just
like that!

From the lone hills where Fergus strays
    Down the long vales of Coonahan
Comes a white wind through the unquiet ways,
    And a tear shall lead the blind man.

But does not this levity jar on me? Yes, it does. I always
want to be on the side of the angels. My wretchedly frequent failure to find definite meanings in the faint and
lovely things of Yeats—my perception of nothing but
some sort of mood enclosed in a vacuum far away—has
always worried me very much. I have repeated sternly and
many times to myself what the initiates have told me:
that through the mouth of Yeats the ancient and authentic
voice of Ireland is uttered. Often I have taken my atlas
from the shelf and looked up Ireland, in search of revelation. And it has seemed to me that if Ireland were indeed
what I there behold, a thing in two dimensions, a design
on paper, and if her counties were not pink and yellow
and green, but all a silvery grey, and if her whole shape
were very much more tenuous and graceful than it is, then
indeed might she be supposed to have some such voice as

Yeats utters. But the fact, of course, is that Ireland, so far from being more rarefied, is grosser than she appears in my atlas. There may be in that land fairies and phantoms, and whispering reeds, and eternal twilight, and wan waters, and tears leading blind men—men, observe! There it is! From time immemorial Ireland has been harbouring human beings. Poetry that hasn't the human note can no more be truly Celtic than it can be truly Saxon or Mongolian or Slav. One is taught to despise Tom Moore nowadays. But I cannot help feeling that in "Ah, believe me when all those endearing young charms" or "One bumper at parting!—tho' many" or "No longer, dear Vesey, feel hurt and uneasy" the ancient spirit of Ireland was more authentically breathed than it is by Yeats. I struggle against this feeling. But in vain.

I often had the pleasure of meeting Yeats, and I liked him. But merely to like so remarkable, so mystic and intense a creature—to be not utterly under his spell whenever one was in his presence—seemed to argue a lack in oneself and to imply an insult to that presence. Thus the pleasure of meeting Yeats was not for me an unmixed one. I felt always rather uncomfortable, as though I had submitted myself to a mesmerist who somehow didn't mesmerise me. I hoped against hope that I should feel my volition slipping away from me—my cheap little independence fading into a drowsy enchantment where visions would come thronging presently. . . . Nothing of the sort happened. . . .

Perhaps because I had formed no expectations, my first sight of Yeats was the deepest impression I had of him. That was in the winter of '93. Aubrey Beardsley had done a poster for the Avenue Theatre and had received two stalls for the first night of Dr. Todhunter's play *The Black Cat*; and he had asked me to go with him. Before the main play there was to be a "curtain-raiser"—*The Land of Heart's Desire*. Yeats was not more than a name to us then; nor were we sure that it beseemed us, as men of the world, to hurry over our dinner. We did so, however, and arrived in good time. The beautiful little play was acted in a very nerveless and inaudible manner, casting rather a gloom over the house. When at length the two curtains of the proscenium swept down and met in the middle of the stage, the applause was fainter than it would be nowadays. There were, however, a few sporadic and compatriotic cries for "Author." I saw a slight convulsion of the curtains where they joined each other, and then I saw a long fissure, revealing (as I for a moment supposed) unlit blackness behind the curtains. But lo! there were two streaks of white in the upper portion of this blackness—a white streak of shirt-front, and above that a white streak of face; and I was aware that what I had thought to be insubstantial murk was a dress-suit, with the Author in it. And the streak of Author's face was partly bisected by a lesser black streak, which was a lock of Author's raven hair. . . . It was all very eerie and memorable.

More than a year passed before his vision was materialised for me in private life. A new publication, entitled *The Savoy*, was afoot, with Arthur Symons for literary editor and Beardsley for art editor. The publisher was a strange and rather depressing person, a north-country-man, known to have been engaged in the sale of disreputable books. To celebrate the first number of the magazine, he invited the contributors to supper in a room at the New Lyric Club. Besides Symons and Beardsley, there were

present Yeats, Mr. Rudolf Dircks, myself, and one or two
other writers whom I forget. Also there was one lady:
the publisher's wife. She had not previously been heard
of by anyone. She was a surprise. She was touching—
dreadfully touching. It was so evident that she had been
brought out from some far suburb for this occasion only.
One knew that the dress she wore had been ordered specially; and one felt that it might never be worn again. She
was small, buxom, and self-possessed. She did the hon-
ours. She dropped little remarks. It did not seem that she
was nervous; one only knew that she *was* nervous. She
knew that she did not matter; but she would not give in;
she was brave and good. Perhaps, if I had not been so pre-
occupied by the pity of her, I would have been more susceptible to Yeats's magic. I wished that I, not he, had been
placed next to her at the table. I could have helped her
more than he. The walls of the little room in which we
supped were lined with bamboo instead of wallpaper.
"Quite original, is it not?" she said to Yeats. But Yeats
had no reply ready for that; only a courteous, lugubrious
murmur. He had been staying in Paris, and was much en-
grossed in the cult of Diabolism, or Devil-worship, which
appeared to have a vogue there. He had made a profound
study of it; and he evidently guessed that Beardsley, whom
he met now for the first time, was a confirmed worshipper
in that line. So to Beardsley he talked, in deep, vibrant
tones across the table, of the lore and rites of Diabolism—
"Dyahbolism" he called it, thereby making it sound the
more fearful. I daresay that Beardsley, who always
seemed to know by instinctive erudition all about everything, knew all about Dyahbolism. Anyhow, I could see
that he, with that stony common-sense which always

came upmost when anyone canvassed the fantastic in him, thought Dyahbolism rather silly. He was too polite not to go on saying at intervals, in his hard, quick voice, "Oh really? How perfectly entrancing!" and "Oh really? How perfectly sweet!" But, had I been Yeats, I would have dropped the subject sooner than he did.

At the other end of the table, Arthur Symons was talking of some foreign city, carrying in his waistcoat-pocket, as it were, the *genius loci,* anon to be embalmed in Pateresque prose. I forget whether this time it was Rome or Seville or Moscow or what; but I remember that the hostess said she had never been there. I liked Symons for feigning some surprise at this, and for saying that she really ought to go. Presently I heard him saying he thought the nomadic life was the best of all lives for an artist. Yeats, in a pause of his own music, heard this too, and seemed a little pained by it. Shaking back the lock from his brow, he turned to Symons and declared that an artist worked best among his own folk and in the land of his fathers. Symons seemed rather daunted, but he stuck to his point. He argued that new sights and sounds and odours braced the whole intelligence of a man and quickened his powers of creation. Yeats, gently but firmly, would have none of this. His own arguments may not have been better than Symons's; but, in voice and manner and countenance, Symons was no match for him at all. And it was with an humane impulse that the hostess interposed.

"Mr. Symons," she said, "is like myself. He likes a little change."

This bathos was so sharp that it was like an actual and visible chasm: one could have sworn to a glimpse of Symons's heels, a faint cry, a thud. Yeats stood for an instant on the brink, stroking his chin engimatically, and then turned to resume the dropped thread of Dyahbolism. I could not help wishing that he, not poor Symons, had been the victim. He would somehow have fallen on his feet; and his voice, issuing uninterruptedly from the depth of the chasm, would have been as impressive as ever.

I have said that my first and merely visual impression of Yeats was my deepest. Do not suppose that at other times he did not impress me with a feeling that I, had I been of finer clay, must have been more deeply impressed than I was. I always did feel that here was *une âme auguste,* if ever there was one. His benign aloofness from whatever company I saw him in, whether he were inspired with language or with silence, made everyone else seem rather cheap. Often, at great receptions in great houses, with colonnaded rooms full of beautiful women in all their jewels, and of eminent men ribanded and starred, it must have seemed to the quietly observant Nobody there that the scene had its final note of distinction in the sober purple soutane of Monsignor So-and-So, yonder. Monsignor So-and-So himself may happen to be as worldly as you will; but nominally, officially, by hierarchic intention, he is apart from the rest. That is the secret of his effect. Something like that was for me the secret of Yeats's effect anywhere. He, not indeed in any nominal or official way, but by reason of himself, was apart from the rest. That was his strength. He was not primarily of this world.

But confound it! So soon as ever one has elaborated a theory, always there is some wretched flaw staring one in the face. Didn't Yeats's management of the Celtic Renascence prove him a practical man? The birth may not have been effected. But there the indefatigable *accoucheur* was. Pamphlets, letters to newspapers, lectures in America, speeches—that speech which I heard him deliver at the Shelbourne Hotel, Dublin; that fighting speech of which George Moore has gasped in *Ave* some slight record for posterity. Yes, it made Moore gasp. Perhaps posterity will be equally stirred. At the Shelbourne Hotel it sounded very beautiful. But no Dons of Trinity, nor any of the Catholics either, were any more offended by it than they would have been by a Nocturne of Chopin. Mournfully, very beautifully, Yeats bombinated in the void, never for an instant in any vital relation to the audience. Moore likens him to Demosthenes. But I take it that Demosthenes swayed multitudes. Yeats swayed Moore. My memory of that speech does somewhat patch the flaw in my theory.

As years went by, the visual aspect of Yeats changed a little. His face grew gradually fuller in outline, and the sharp angles of his figure were smoothed away; and his hands—those hands which in his silences lay folded downward across his breast, but left each other and came forth and, as it were, stroked the air to and fro while he talked —those very long, fine hands did seem to have lost something of their insubstantiality. His dignity and his charm were as they had always been. But I found it less easy to draw caricatures of him. He seemed to have become subtly less like himself.

(WRITTEN 1914)

H. B. IRVING AS A YOUNG MAN

[SUNDAY, 2 JANUARY 1955]

LADIES AND GENTLEMEN, almost forty years ago I wrote, but didn't publish, a few little essays about meetings with interesting contemporaries of mine. One of these essays was about my two first meetings with H. B. Irving— Harry Irving, the elder son of Sir Henry, and father of Mr. Laurence Irving, whose biography of Sir Henry is assuredly the vividest and best that any actor has ever had.

This little essay I will now read to you.

In the autumn of 1890 I was a freshman at Merton College, Oxford. I was a year younger than most of the other freshmen, and was young even for my age. Except in my very last term at school I had been wearing Eton collars. I was not yet accustomed to collars that stood up. I was a child. Not so, far from so, in his third year at New College, was Harry Irving.

It was young George Bancroft who presented me to him. He too, in his way, seemed to me very wonderful. He was so finished and formed—so perfect a little man of the world; a perfect miniature, both in face and in costume, of his father, Sir Squire Bancroft. But he did not frighten me. His eyes had the famous twinkle of his mother's, and they had twinkled very kindly on me when he came to call on me and to invite me to breakfast with him on the following Sunday. He was a Brasenose man, was in his third year, and had lodgings in St. Giles. "I'll ask Harry Irving and some other fellows," he said, in quite a casual tone.

Two or three of the other fellows were already there when I arrived; and two or three others followed. I was presented to them all. They seemed very tall and easy and important, and I thought it impossible that they would remember me if they saw me again. George Bancroft wore a smoking-jacket with quilted facings of blue silk. This summed up for me the possibilities of adult grandeur and emancipation. It was the symbol of all that a Sunday morning at school was not. Yet anon it was to be as naught in my eyes—it and the man in it, and all those other men. For anon the door flew open: in, with the bent strut of his father, came H. B. Irving.

As he crossed the threshold, he said in a deep voice, "Ha!" He clapped a hand on Bancroft's shoulder, rather in the manner of a very eminent detective arresting a very unimportant thief. Then, with that hand still on that shoulder, he distributed nods and "Ha!'s" among the company—the company of "supers." His gaze alighted on *me*.

"This," said Bancroft (with the pride of a "super" who has a line to speak), "is Mr. Beerbohm, of Merton."

"Ha!" He had a way of looking at one through his

pince-nez, less intimidating only than a way he had of looking at one *over* his pince-nez. "Ha!" he repeated. And then, "A brother of Beerbohm Tree, aren't you?"

"A half-brother," I said faintly.

"Ha!"

It was as though he had said "That may or may not be an extenuating circumstance, I will consider it."

We were to have breakfast downstairs. Bancroft led the way. The others instinctively let Irving go out next. I felt I was almost on terms of equality with these others now, and found myself talking quite glibly to one of them on the way down.

Our host was at the head of the table—topographically. But spiritually and truly, and to all intents and purposes, the head of any table at which H. B. Irving seated himself was just where H. B. Irving sat. I do not remember much that he said; he may not even have said much; but his manner was such that anything said by him had at the moment the effect of a Standard Work condensed by him for the occasion. The name of a well-known public man was mentioned by somebody. Irving seemed for a moment to search his memory. "I once met him at supper," he said, "at my father's." Just that. No more. But it somehow —by some miracle of cadence and glance and eyebrow— implied an adverse and irrevocable judgment. That well-known man had been paraded, inspected, seen through, dismissed: the less said about him the better. And moreover, as I was to find, there always was in H. B. Irving's way of saying "my father" something which brought to bear on one suddenly and personally the full weight of the Lyceum tradition. True, he always carried that weight around with him, as it were, but it seemed to come down on one with special force whenever "my father" was mentioned.

It was as "Young Irving" that he was always spoken of by the undergraduates at large. The adjective seemed rather ill-chosen, but it implied no disrespect. As was Old Irving's fame in Great Britain and America, so was Young Irving's in Oxford. In the year before I matriculated he had appeared as King John in Shakespeare's play, and had been highly praised by the many critics who travelled down from London to see him. If not perhaps one of the most eloquent speakers at the Union, he was certainly the most impressive. He had made a special study, too, of Judge Jeffreys, and had read a paper about him to more than one Essay Society. And he was a student of Criminology, and was to practise at the Criminal Bar when he "went down." Walking up the High, "Look," one undergraduate would say to another, "there goes Young Irving," and in Hall that evening he would say "I saw Young Irving in the High today." Young Irving's rooms were in Radcliffe Square, and it was natural that he should pass often up and down the High on his way to and from them; but the sight of him was never taken as a matter of course. It was always something to have just seen him. And oh—to have just met him at breakfast! I wonder to how many of my fellow freshmen at Merton did I in the course of that memorable Sunday say, as lightly as I could, "I met Young Irving at breakfast this morning."

I knew now, after this face-to-face meeting, that the lightness of Bancroft's "Harry Irving and some other fellows" had been a histrionic assumption. I hoped I was carrying off my own assumption equally well. I tried to make my eyes twinkle in the Bancroft manner. But I think they were yet obviously the eyes of a child who had been frightened.

What a terror to witnesses was lost by Young Irving's abandonment of the Law! True, the days of Sergeant Parry and Sergeant Ballantyne were no more. The tone of the Old Bailey had already been dulcified to that pitch of suavity and ruth which is the key-note of our modern life. Young Irving would have somewhat restored the fine old traditions, showing even from under his stuff-gown the ermine of Judge Jeffreys. Perhaps, ere the time came for him to exchange stuff for silk, he would have mellowed. For he did within a few years delightfully mellow; and it may be not really so wonderful as I like to think— not such a sign of later powers developed in myself—that I achieved the habit of calling him "Harry." But not at Oxford did the mellowing process begin. And when, one day, I received an invitation to lunch in Radcliffe Square, I quaked as at the service of a writ, and was gratified as by a royal command.

The summons was for the following day. I read it several times. Then I leaned out from my ground-floor window, deeply inhaling. A fellow freshman was crossing the quadrangle. I greeted him: "Can you lunch with me tomorrow? Oh no, by-the-by, not tomorrow: tomorrow I've got to lunch with Young Irving. The day *after* tomorrow?"

Within an hour or so, by repetition of this formula, I had accumulated quite a large party for the day after tomorrow. I forget whether it went off well. I remember only the previous day.

It had not struck me that Irving and I might be alone.
Else, I might hardly have dared to accept. Down went
my heart like lead in water when, punctually presenting
myself on the threshold of his room, I saw, together with
my vision of his back awfully silhouetted against the bow-
window, covers laid for two. Covers? I knew that I could
not hide under my plate.

Probably I uttered a cough, for I remember the sud-
denness with which the silhouette veered round and said
"Ha!" to me.

I daresay that you, like me, often at important junc-
tures think suddenly of some outrageous thing that you
might do, and of the appalling results there would be if
you did it—results so appalling that for an instant, in
your horror, you feel that you actually *have* done the
thing. There was for me a gruesome instant in which I
felt that I had actually said "Ha!" back to Irving.

The relief of finding that I had not done so seemed to
inspire me with a sort of jaunty confidence. I found myself
quite articulate—indeed, fluent! At school I had been
thought clever. "Has natural abilities of a rare order"—
this phrase from a form-master's Report came floating
into my brain. Why should I not impress myself on Irving
today as a man with abilities of a rare order? He seemed
to be inclined to draw me out. Let him be astonished with
the draft. Let him get more than he bargained for. I
thought of David and Goliath. But—what if Goliath had
looked at David over his pince-nez as Irving looked at
me over his? I felt that what I babbled was in no way remarkable. I felt I had no abilities of *any* order. That
form-master had been a fool. So was I. Already, though

luncheon had hardly begun, I was seen through, over that pince-nez. I was asked many questions, to which I gave the feeblest and most rambling answers, foreseeing all the while one question which especially I dreaded. Perhaps, thought I, hoping against hope, this question would not be put. But at the end of the meal came a silence which I knew could terminate in only one way. Irving had risen from the table and offered me a cigar. Never having smoked a cigar, I took a cigarette. Irving cut and lit a cigar for himself, motioned me to an arm-chair, flung himself on the sofa, propped his elbow on the back of it, propped his brow on his hand, and over his pince-nez looked at me. "And what," he asked, "are you going to do in after-life?"

"Well," I said—and the poor monosyllable came out as a polysyllabic bleat, "we-e-e-e-ell," after which the other poor words came out in three separate gasps sped by a weak smile—"as a matter of fact I'm—I'm thinking of—being called to the Bar."

And these words, at the very moment of utterance, became untrue. I *had*, up to that moment, vaguely destined myself for the Bar. But in expressing to Irving this ambition, I saw the full absurdity of it and for good and all dropped it before he had time to say (as he did with more than his usual gravity say) "Ha!" My weak smile, my gasps, the blush burning my brow, had forced this plain moral on me: I was *not* for the Forum. I suppose that in any case I would have discovered this truth for myself fairly soon; but the fact remains that I discovered it then and there by stress of Irving's presence. I did not let him know this. I was too proud to say "But please, Sir, I've just changed my mind, I'm not for the Forum—oh no,

Sir! The Forum's for you, Sir!" Indeed, I rather resented his power over me; and so glad, presently, was I to be out on the door-step in Radcliffe Square that I not merely could have danced: I did, actually dance. . . . I was only a child, remember.

(WRITTEN 1914)

HETHWAY SPEAKING

[Sunday, 25 December 1955]

L ADIES AND GENTLEMEN, in 1895 I, who was then a
very young man, made acquaintance with a far older
one, Mr. Sylvester Hethway. He lived in a beautiful old
house in Cheyne Walk. He was a man of keen literary and
artistic taste, and in the eighteen-sixties and 'seventies had
been a friend of many men whose names had magic for
my young ears. Of them and of their characters he was
very ready to talk to me, and I would afterwards write
out, as exactly in his own words as I could remember
them, what he had told me.

Some weeks ago, in a cupboard, I came across a few
of these old reports; and it has been thought that you
might be interested to hear some of them.

Here, then, is Hethway speaking of Swinburne as Swinburne had been at the time when George Meredith and

he lodged in the house of Dante Gabriel Rossetti further along Cheyne Row.

"Ah, Swinburne, yes. Strange little creature. He had the prettiest, funniest ways. He was wonderfully endearing. Apart from his genius, he was the most childlike of little children. One did so want no harm to come to him. And he was so anxious to be good and obedient. But he hadn't will-power enough for that. He caused us all the greatest anxiety. What could be done? It wasn't that he drank much wine, but that so very little of it went to his head—and that he did always want a little. I fancy that somehow he *needed* it, too. It wasn't good for his body; but then, you see, his body was such an infinitesimal part of him: the rest was all spirit; and the spirit perhaps required a special diet. It was all very odd. Everything about Swinburne was odd. Meredith used to call him Algernon the Incalculable. 'It's maddening,' he would say, 'to find anyone making so much out of—nothing. How does he do it? We other fellows have to go through a long process of doing and *being,* and then of thinking hard about what we've done and what we are. We have to go to and fro, gathering faggots for tinder; laboriously and cunningly we stack them—and *then,* as likely as not, they won't burn. But Swinburne can always make a blaze without a speck of fuel. There's nothing *in* him but inspiration. *Our* main difficulty is how to make a beginning: his only problem is how to leave off.'

"Another time, Meredith said, 'It's all very well to say that Algernon gets his motive-power from books, not from life. It's true, but it's not the whole truth. If all the books in the world were burnt tomorrow, and nothing left of them but one charred corner of a page from an old

French chronicle, Algernon would find enough in that to enable him to go on creating for ever.' "

Hethway told me that Rossetti, the very sedentary Rossetti, found Meredith, with his great love of wind and weather, rather a trial. Rossetti had said one day dolefully, "He's always coming in early in the afternoon, just as I'm beginning to paint well.—'Glorious weather, Rossetti!' he cries. 'Come out for a stretch with me—do you all the good in the world!' He always seems to be going to Hendon, and he always brings out the name as though it were a name to conjure with—something sacred, irresistible; Mecca; the Promised Land.—I say to him, Meredith, if you brought Hendon to me in your hand, I wouldn't look at it.—Or I say, Look here, my dear fellow: this is an easel, this is a canvas, this is a palette, and this is *me*—just getting into my stride. Go and get into yours, by all means. *I* don't ask you to sit down and help me paint this picture. Why should you want me to assist you in trapesing to Hendon? Once and for all, Meredith, Hendon be damned!—For a moment he has a puzzled look, then he throws back his head, laughs that great laugh of his, and swings out of the studio, banging the door behind him. I never dare ask him not to bang the door, because then he'd tell me that if I took exercise I shouldn't have nerves. And I should have to explain that I'd much rather jump an inch or two off my chair than walk ten miles or whatever the confounded distance to Hendon is."

Hethway had seen a fair amount of Thomas Carlyle. He said: "One day, when I had been travelling abroad, I went in to see him. He told me he had been painted by a young Mr. James Whistler. It was an odd conjunction. I

asked him how it had come about. He said it was through
Madame Venturi. I daresay you've never heard of her.
She had lived for many years in Chelsea. She was a great
friend of dear Mrs. Carlyle. Both these ladies had an immense esteem for Mazzini, whom Carlyle thought a poor
crittur—not because Mazzini was so, but because Carlyle
was so unvarying in his judgment of men. . . . Since
Mrs. Carlyle's death he had formed the habit of going often to Madame Venturi's house. He may have thought her
a poor crittur, but she loved Janie's memory, and that sufficed. 'And one day,' he told me, 'there was a wee young
man with a mop of black ringlets and a quizzing-glass—
a sor-rt of pocket D'Israeli by the looks of him, but American in his talk, of which there was much. When he was
gone, Mrs. Venturi asked me what I thought of him; and
I told her without cir-r-cumlocution. Said she, But he's
going to be a verra great painter, and he wants to paint
you; and he's verra poor, she said: and he's verra guid to
his Mither-r. She's a most per-rtinaceous crittur, is Mrs.
Venturi, and next day I found myself with her at a house
alongside the river, there to see this Mr. Whistler's paintings. The Mither-r received us—a dainty-sad little auld
silvery dame, gentle of speech and shy-authoritative. Presently in comes son, and we all go into his wor-rk-room,
and there, propped up on a bit of wooden stand, is a picture of the Mither-r, with a frame to it. There she sat, side-
face, a sad figure, all in black, lonesome and shy-authoritative, against a plain grey wall of parlour. I canna count
how many sittings I gave that slow-working son. One day
he said finis and showed me his handiwork. There I sat,
side-face, all in black, lonesome and meditative-gentle,

against pale grey wall of parlour. Painter stood by me sharp-expectant. "Well, young man," I said at last, "ye're verra filial, verra filial indeed." ' "

Of William Morris at the time when he had founded with his friend Faulkner the famous firm of furnishers and decorators, Hethway gave me an interesting glimpse: "One morning Pringle, my butler, came up to my study and said that Mr. Faulkner and another gentleman were in the drawing-room. He said, 'I told Mr. Faulkner you were not at home, sir, but the other gentleman said that then they'd come in and wait.' I asked Pringle who the other gentleman was. 'I don't know, sir,' he said. 'A seafaring gentleman, I think.' I wondered what Morris could want with me.

"As I went downstairs I heard his voice raised in great enthusiasm about something, and, as I entered, the sturdy and rosy fellow rushed at me and clapped me on the shoulders. 'Splendid,' he cried, stepping back, 'grandiose, scrumptious.'

" 'What is?' I asked.

" 'Why, this,' he answered, spinning round on his heel, with his right arm extended, and radiantly facing me again.

" 'You like the room?' I asked.

" 'Like it? Why, it's the most beautiful room in London.'

"I turned to Faulkner (who was standing in the background—looking, I noticed, rather uncomfortable) and 'Well,' I said, 'this *is* praise indeed from Sir Hubert! I was afraid Morris wouldn't approve of my taste at all. This sofa, for instance—very different from that famous wooden settle of his in Red Lion Square.'

" 'Sofa?' cried Morris. 'Call that a sofa? Why it's only a—a perch for canary-birds. But the *room*—Golly!' and he spun ecstatically round on his heel, upsetting this time a slim Sheraton stand on which was a silver vase with a rose in it. 'Sorry,' he exclaimed, picked up the stand, re-placed the vase and the rose, and—he was always extraor-dinarily handy—mopped the wet floor dry with his huge handkerchief; all in an instant of time. 'Sorry,' he said again, 'but it's the gimcrack's own fault, you know. And it clinches our scheme, by Jove, doesn't it?'

" 'What scheme?' I inquired.

" 'Oh, I forgot: you weren't in the room. *The* scheme. To make a clean sweep of all these folderols and really *furnish* the room. Moment I came in, I swore we'd do this *for* you—didn't I, Faulkner? We'd been round to see Gabriel Rossetti, on business. As we came away Faulkner pointed out this house to me—told me you lived here. Confess I'd quite forgotten you, old chap. Liked the look of your house, though. Thought you might want some things. Besides: pleasure to see you again. Wasn't pre-pared for this room, though. Felt the challenge of it at once. I've got half the designs in my head already, and I'll put 'em in hand today. All you've got to do is to get your things carted off to Christie's or somewhere and pocket what they fetch. I and Faulkner and Co. will do the rest.'

"I said, 'Your idea is that I should sell all that I have and follow you?'

" 'Right!—you've hit it,' he cried. 'And what's more, we'll let you have everything at two per cent above cost of production, by Jiminy, because we're blooming beginners and you're our friend. Hooray! I've got *all* the designs in my head now,' and he struck his forehead a violent blow with his fist. 'I see your whole blesséd room for you, all clear before me. You shall have a great cedar chair—*there,* in the middle—like Odin's throne; and a settle—all along *this* wall—to seat a regiment. And Ned Burne-Jones will do the stained glass for your windows—Life of La Belle Iseult; and Ford Madox Brown shall do the panels of the settle—Boyhood of Chaucer; and'—he strode up and down, brandishing his arms—'there's a young chap named William De Morgan who'll do the tiles for the hearth; and my wife shall embroider the edges of the window-curtains—you know that green serge we've got, Faulkner—glorious. And by Jove we'll'—but here he slipped and sat with a terrific crash on the parquet. 'That's just what I was going to speak about,' he continued, sitting; 'this isn't a floor, it's a sheet of ice: it won't do; we must have good honest rough oaken boards with bulrushes,' he cried, bounding to his feet, '—strewn bulrushes. And we'll have a—'

" 'One moment, Morris,' I begged. 'When you say *we,* do you mean simply yourself and Faulkner and the Company, or do you include *me?*'

" 'But of course I include you, he said. 'Why, hang it all, the *room*'s yours.'

" 'That's just what I was beginning to doubt,' I said.

"He stared hard at me, and I at him. Rather a dog-and-cat effect, I suppose. It lasted some seconds. Morris saw that I wouldn't waver. One of his great qualities was that he never wasted time. He always concentrated his energies on things that *could* be done, he never repined over things that couldn't. Here was a thing that couldn't. He looked at his watch, whistled (he always whistled whenever he looked at his watch), snatched his hat—'Come

along, Faulkner!' he cried. 'No offence, Hethway!'—and
was gone.

"He was a queer fellow—a great character; quite apart.
And as good as gold. But I hadn't much in common with
him."

Of course Hethway's friends and acquaintances were
not all members of the Rossettian and Chelsean circle. He
had been privileged to know Tennyson, for instance, and
had met repeatedly the very social Robert Browning. Here
is a contrast he drew between those two:

"They were as unlike their own work as they were unlike each other. When I think of them I am tempted to
say that a man's work is rather the needful supplement to
himself than the mere outcome of it—or at any rate that
the smoothness of a man's art is in inverse ratio to his own.
The smoother Tennyson's verse became, the more rugged
and tangled was he to look at. The more tangled and rugged Browning made his poetry, the more surely would
anyone meeting him for the first time have taken him for a
banker, or a fashionable physician. The greater the exac-
tions he made, as he grew older, on the intellect and the
patience of his readers, the easier was it to understand what
he said—and even to foretell what he *would* say—at a din-
ner-table. And Tennyson's manners—ah, they were the
very least of all adapted to courtly circles at the very time
when he had finally purged his art of anything that might
conceivably vex the ghost of the Prince Consort."

And here finally is the report I made of what Hethway one day had to say about Walter Pater:

"He would come and see me here sometimes. He had a
house with his sisters in Earl's Terrace—Kensington, you
know. But he didn't like Kensington very much. He used

to say, 'The High Street is so full of noise and stress.' He liked Cheyne Walk. I remember his standing with me at a window here in this room, one day in Spring, gazing out silently. A tug passed by, towing a couple of barges. 'One might almost wish,' he said in his gentle voice, 'that the river could be exempt from traffic. *It does, a little, mar your secular peace.*' I laughed outright, and I think Miss Pater, who had come with him, was rather shocked by my mirth; but not so Pater; he liked to be amiably rallied, to be teased a little, by his friends. I met him somewhere a few days later, and told him that his remark had been re-peated by me to the River Police, and that they, being men of some culture and great admirers of his prose style, had said to me, 'When next Mr. Pater is coming to see you, sir, please let us know. We will stop the traffic.'

"For chaff of that kind he had a keen relish. I don't know whether you young men read him much? I believe that at Oxford in the 'seventies and 'eighties and perhaps even in your own time he had quite a following and was taken very seriously as a teacher. I myself have never been able to take teachers or preachers *very* seriously. Of course I have often admired the genius, the force, or grace, of this one and that. But their actual 'messages' are —well, they're so very characteristic of the messengers: the vain ones who want us to be just like themselves; and the modest ones who would have us be just what they are not. I have known many messengers, and all fall into one or the other of these two categories. Mr. Carlyle, with all his faults of temper, was one of the modest kind, and Mr. Ruskin—generous and usually angelic though he was—one of the vain. Mr. Carlyle, being eloquent, and a peasant, and always ailing, desiderated a race of strong silent aristocrats; and dear Mr. Ruskin despaired of a world in which not everybody admired Giotto and Turner and Miss Kate Greenaway so much as he. Great men, both of them; but great not in their messages, great in their *delivery*. Dear Matthew Arnold—Matt Arnold, as we called him—was not quite on their level, of course; but he had a great vogue, he was very much listened to in the 'seventies. *His* hope for the English upper and middle and lower classes was that they should all with one accord read Sophocles and Goethe. He was, I am afraid, pre-eminently one of the vain. Among the modest there was no more shining light than Walter Pater. He earnestly counselled the young to be—what was the famous phrase?—to 'be present always at the focus where the greatest number of vital forces unite in their purest energy.' And he himself could not stand Kensington High Street. He very solemnly warned the young that 'to form habits is failure in life.' I suggested to him one day that in the next edition of his book he ought to add a foot-note: 'In life, however, there are worse things than failure: for example, not having one's cup of tea, with a slice of thin bread and butter, at five o'clock *punctually*.' He laughed gently and said, 'That is a shrewd jest at *me*, Hethway; but not at the sincerity of my doctrine.' And of course he was quite right there. No man was more sincere in his efforts to make people as unlike himself as possible. His one lapse from constancy was when he urged them 'to burn always with a hard, gem-like flame.' To burn like that, one must shut out all draughts, as *he* did. One must burn inside a small closed lantern, as *he* did . . . as *I* do, I suppose, nowadays," Hethway added, with a smile. "But I don't regard myself as a terrible example—nor as a good one. In fact, I've no message for the world."

And, indeed, he had none. For he existed, let me now confess, only in my imagination and in the intention I had many years ago to write a book around him—a book to be entitled *The Mirror of the Past*, a mirror which, hanging in his drawing-room, gradually ceased to reflect present things and began to reflect things long past. I had made many notes for such a book; and among them were those notes of Hethway's conversation which I have just been reading to you. Please don't be vexed with me for having let you suppose Sylvester was a real person. I thought that he as a real person would be likelier than I as a fabricator to impress and please you. Ladies and Gentlemen, goodnight.

AN INCIDENT

[THURSDAY, 14 JUNE 1956]

ONE AFTERNOON in the early Spring of (I think) the year 1906, I took part, with Henry James, in an incident which afterwards seemed to me strangely and exactly like the basis of a short story written by himself— one of the many stories he wrote on the theme of an elderly and very eminent great writer in relation to an earnest young admirer and disciple.

I had been at a luncheon party given by Somerset Maugham at the Carlton Hotel, and I was on my way to my club, the Savile, which in those days was housed at the southern end of Piccadilly. A new monthly review had just been started, with a story in it by Henry James—a story entitled "The Velvet Glove." I was going straight to the Savile to read that story. There was a keen north-easterly wind blowing, and I was wearing a rather thin overcoat, and was therefore walking quickly. But I would have been speeding in any case, so eager was I to read that story. And then, half-way down the slope, I encountered a slowly ascending figure that seemed to me vaguely familiar. I must explain that hitherto it was only in drawing-rooms and dining-rooms that I had seen Henry James, and that his magnificently massive and shapely brow was what had always most impressed me there. Hence my momentary failure now to recognise him in a very large old top hat of which the brim came down almost to the level of his eyebrows. He, however, had identified *me* and he accosted me in the deeply ruminating manner that was his. He told me he had just come up to London from his home at Rye. He said he was "to all intents and purposes a country cousin," and he asked me whether there was any new exhibition of pictures for him to see. I was able to tell him that there was a very good one at the Grafton Galleries. He asked me, with much circumlocution, whether I would be inclined to act as his guide. I felt much honoured—and yet, to my great surprise, I heard myself saying instantly "Well, I'm afraid I can't. I have to be in Kensington at half-past three." "Ah," he said, "you young men, always entangled in webs of engagements, yes, yes . . ." and passed on up the slope.

What had prompted me to tell that fib? It wasn't merely the north-east wind and the thin overcoat and the prospect of having to walk slowly up that slope. It wasn't merely shyness and the fear that whatever I might have to say would seem cheap and tawdry to Henry James, that profoundly fastidious critic of men. Nor was it merely the presentiment that he would not share my admiration for that picture which was the outstanding one in the Grafton Galleries—young Augustus John's "Woman Smiling." It was mainly my aforesaid impatience to be reading "The Velvet Glove."

And here I was now in the Savile, reading it. It was, of course, a very good story, and yet, from time to time, I found my mind wandering away from it. It was not so characteristic, not so intensely Jamesian a story as James would have founded on the theme of what had just been happening between us—the theme of a disciple loyally—or unloyally?—preferring the Master's work to the Master.

(WRITTEN 1954)

Other Things

A NOTE ON THE EINSTEIN
THEORY

I T IS SAID THAT THERE ARE, besides Dr. Einstein himself, only two men who can claim to have grasped the Theory in full. I cannot claim to be either of these. But I do know a good thing when I see it; and here is a thing that is excellent in its kind—romantically excellent in a kind that is itself high. When I think of rays being deflected by gravity, and of parallel lines at long last converging so that there isn't perhaps, after all, any such thing as Infinity, I draw a very deep breath indeed. The attempt to conceive Infinity had always been quite arduous enough for me. But to imagine the absence of it; to feel that perhaps we and all the stars beyond our ken are somehow cosily (though awfully) closed in by curtain curves beyond which is nothing; and to convince myself, by the way, that this exterior nothing is not (in virtue of *being* nothing) something, and therefore . . . but I lose the thread.

Enough that I never lose the thrill. It excites, it charms me to think of elderly great mathematicians of this and that nation packing their portmanteaus whenever there is to be a solar eclipse, and travelling over land and sea to the Lick Observatory, or to some hardly accessible mountain-top in Kamchatka, and there testing, to the best of their power, the soundness or unsoundness of the tremendous Theory. So far, the weather has not been very favourable to these undertakings. Nature, who is proud and secretive, has opposed many clouds to the batteries of telescopes. But she has had only a partial success, it seems. Some observations have been more or less clearly made, some conclusions more or less clearly drawn. And these more or less clearly point to the likelihood that what Dr. Einstein in his humdrum home evolved from his inner consciousness is all delightfully correct.

But is the British public delighted? It gives no sign of being so. Its newspapers did at the first news of Einstein's existence try, very honourably, to excite it about Einstein and even about his work. It would *not* be excited. Strange! The tamest batting of Hertfordshire *v.* Australia, the feeblest goal-keeping of Wormwood Scrubbs *v.* Hornsey Rise, the lightest word that falls from the lips of the least accomplished Negro boxer, are better "copy" than any challenge to our notion of the Cosmos. This is all the stranger because the public is not careless of other things than Sport. Its passionate interest in archaeology, for instance, rose to boiling-point, only the other day: it could *not* hear too much about the tomb of Tutankhamen, nor tire of debating whether or not the bones of that king might rightly be disturbed. Why never a word as to the disturbance of our belief that parallel lines can nowhere converge? I haven't grudged Tutankhamen the renewal and immense enlargement of the fame he once had. I have but deplored the huge cold shoulder turned on the living Einstein.

Newton, no greater an innovator than he, is popular enough. Everybody knows something about Gravitation—and all about the apple. Perhaps if Newton had not mentioned that apple, he too would be generally ignored. It is a great advantage for a discoverer to have been inspired by some homely little incident. Newton and the apple, Copernicus and the whipping-top, James Watt and the kettle. But Einstein and——? Poor Einstein!

Men of his magnitude are not avid of popularity? True; but this does not mean that popularity would be disagreeable to them. When the newspapers were trying to make Relativity a household word, I read an account of Einstein, written by one who knew him, and enhanced by a photograph of him. A very human person, I gathered; far from stand-offish; a player of the fiddle; the constant smoker of a large pipe; a genial, though thoughtful, critic of current things. I liked his views on education. Why all this forcing of a child's memory? Memory—a matter of little moment. Let the child be taught to see, and to think, for itself. And let every child be taught a trade. And "after all," said Einstein, dismissing tuition, "the best thing in the world is a happy face." It was clear from the photograph that his own face was a happy one. But I discerned in it a certain wistfulness, too—the wistfulness of a thorough good fellow whose work somehow repels the attention of that good fellow, the average man. My heart went out to him. I wished I could help him. And now, I think, I can. Hark!

Yesterday afternoon I was walking on the coast-road from Rapallo to Zoagli when I saw approaching in the distance a man of strenuous gait, and of aspect neither Italian nor English. His brow was bare to the breeze; and as he drew near I perceived the brow to be a fine one; and as he drew nearer still I perceived the face to be a very happy one—with just a hint in it of wistfulness, which, however, vanished at my words, "Dr. Einstein, I presume?" He clapped a cordial hand on my shoulder; he treated me as an old friend, as a brother, and insisted that we should sit together on the low wall that divides the road from the cliff. Presently—after he had praised the sun and the sea, and had expressed an ardent sympathy with Fascismo, and with Socialismo, no less—I said to him, "Master (if one who is not a disciple may so address you), tell me: What was it that first put you on the track of the tremendous Theory?" He knitted his fine brow, saying that his memory was not a very good one; but after a while he remembered, and spoke to me as follows:

"One winter's evening, after a hard day's work, I was sitting by my fireside—for I have an open fire in the English fashion, not a stove: I like to sit watching the happy faces in the coals—when my eye lighted on the tongs in the fender. Of course it had often lighted on them before; but this time it carried to my brain a message which my brain could not understand. 'Here,' I mused, 'are two perfectly parallel lines. And yet, and yet, they meet at the extreme ends. How is that?' My friend Professor Schultz had promised to drop in and smoke a pipe with me that evening, and when he came I drew his attention to the phenomenon. He knelt down by the fender, pushed his spectacles up on to his forehead, gazed closely, and muttered, 'Gott im Himmel—ja!' I asked him—for he is a very ready man—if he had any explanation to offer. He rose from his knees and sat down on a chair heavily, burying his head in his hands. Suddenly he sprang to his feet. 'Einstein,' he said, 'I believe I have it! I believe that the iron-worker who made those bars must have heated them red-hot and then bent the ends towards each other.' Dear old Schultz! Always so ready!—so shallow! I suppose I ought not to have laughed; but I did; and Schultz went out in some anger. It was dawn when I rose from the fireside. The fire had long ago burnt itself out, and I was stiff with cold. But my mind was all aglow with the basic principles of Relativismus."

"The world," I said quietly, "shall hear of this, Dr. Einstein."

1923

FROM BLOOMSBURY
TO BAYSWATER

IN AUGUST 1935 it seemed that we might at any moment be at war with Italy, a country in which I had resided for many years. Accordingly I returned to the land of my birth and heart; and the stormy petrel, partly by chance, and partly for good reasons of economy, folded its wings in Bloomsbury, and was there for rather more than a year.

Tavistock Square is not so fine a place as Bedford Square or Brunswick Square; but it is (as you will already have guessed) a Square, and has therefore much to be said for it. Very greatly did I enjoy the charm of seeing through my two large windows on the ground-floor the gradual turn of the leaf, the yellowing and the browning of it, its fall, its wind-swept eddying along the road; and the austere nakedness of the great old trees, offering a distant view of the houses on the other side, and of the omnibuses that passed incessantly along that unhappy other side and blessedly couldn't be heard on ours; and in due time the clean snow upon the grass and upon the soot-black but noble branches; and later the small green buds that are so much stranger than on country trees; and gradually the disappearance of the inaudible omnibuses and of the windows of the unblest; and then again the yellowing and the browning, the falling and the eddying. It is in a city, surely, that the lover of Nature finds deepest pleasure in watching her old round of phases.

Nevertheless, he prefers the country; and I am sure that in the eighteenth century I should have wished to murder that Duke of Bedford who for purposes of pelf had his great house demolished, and his park and his fields innumerable built over by a bright young architect and surveyor. I should not have realised that the architecture was good. I should have taken its manner as a matter of course. The spaciousness and solidity and homely grandeur of it all, the generous width of its doors and doorsteps and of its areas, would have won no word of praise from my pursed-up lips. Nor would the correspondingly generous width of the roads and of the pavements have surprised and mollified me. One lives and learns. One lives another century and a half and begins to appreciate.

In my youth Bloomsbury meant little to me. It didn't— it doesn't even now—appeal to the historic sense. Such places as St. James's and Westminster and Mayfair had always had shining inmates: such places were of the centre, and near the rose. Bloomsbury in its day was much favoured by eminent lawyers, and by their wives and families. And outside their courts lawyers mostly burn with but a dim light. Moreover, they had deserted Bloomsbury before I was born, leaving their houses to the letters of lodgings and to the keepers of boarding-houses, or even to emptiness and darkness, or even to disrepute. If Bloomsbury had vanished utterly, my young heart would not have mourned it. But now it *is* beginning to vanish little by little. Many of the Squares and Streets have been more or less vandalised. All of them are threatened. I gather that the arch-threatener is the University of London. I understand that there are no limits to its desire for expansion of that bleak, blank, hideous, and already vast whited sepulchre which bears its name. Simultaneous tens of thousands of youths and maidens yet unborn will in the not so very far distant future be having their minds filled there and their souls starved there. Poor things! (And I'm sorry for the dons too.)

To them, perhaps, what may remain of the present Bloomsbury will have that historic interest which for us it lacks. They may say to one another, "In that small brown house yonder, Henry Smith wrote his immortal 'Snarls,' " and "In that one, Philip Robinson painted some of the most exquisitely unsightly of his dissignifications." For of course, since 1918 or so, Bloomsbury has got into inverted commas, and has (though Philip Robinson will blame me for using the word) a meaning. It has become an intellectual centre, or, as it would call itself (for it is very Russian in its leanings), a focus of the intelligentsia. I myself am not *very* Russian, and to me the term "intelligentsia" seems less modest and less apt than "mental underworld." Dostoievsky, their god, was a man of genius, certainly, and gave beautifully poignant expression to his spinelessness. But he is altogether alien to our rough island race; and laborious little imitations of his inspired maunderings cut no ice, and win scant patience from the average reader, even if they are contrived in all deep reverence to the memory of Karl Marx, and in fond though violent indigestion of the theories of Dr. Freud. But here I am presuming an average reader able to elucidate those tricksy snippets of dry prose in which the poetry of the West Central young is written. Here am I forgetting that intelligibility is as darkly frowned on by these young as are those stuffy old fads of the Victorian bourgeoisie, beauty, harmony, movement, development, and similar rot that had been handed down from the dark ages of Periclean Athens and had loathsomely imposed itself on generation after craven generation of the cloddish human race, and was seen through and discarded only as a result of the European War of 1914–1918.

Certainly that war was a bad time to be born in, and the subsequent years must have been unhappy ones to grow up in. I daresay that were I a young man of the period I too should be disgruntled. I was fortunate in the (almost pre-historic) date of my birth. Even so, however, I was foolish enough in my youth, as is the way of young men. But I wonder whether, if I were young now, I should be quite such a fool as to suppose that literary or graphic artists can advantageously forgo the influence of tradition and start with quite clean slates. The world has been going on for ever so long, with ever so many gifted people in it. Anything that is worth doing has been done frequently. Things hitherto undone should be given, I suspect, a wide berth. Let the young rise in revolt, from time to time, by all means. But, to be fruitful, their revolts must be, in another sense, from time to time: from the present to the past. In the nineteenth century there were two movements of importance; one of them a revolt from the formalism of the previous century, the other from the current fashions of academic art. But Romance was, after all, an old and familiar affair; nor were Giotto and his kind imaginary figures. The only novelty was the style in which the old ways were handled and developed and extended in the new period. The Impressionists? For the moment, I was forgetting them. But they are no snag. None of my Chelsea friends of the 'nineties supposed Manet to have been a phoenix. Steer and Sickert, MacColl and Will Rothenstein were all vocally aware of kings before Agamemnon—Spanish, Italian, and other kings.

I wonder that the Chelsea of those days could have slipped my memory, so obvious is the contrast of it with the Bloomsbury of these!—so fresh and tonic was the air of it; so gay were the artists of that village (for village it still seemed to be) by the riverside. Why hasn't Bloomsbury a river?—a cheering, strong-flowing river, washing things away to the sea. I feel sure that even in the interbella period a river would have done Bloomsbury no end of good. Regent's Park is very airy, and isn't very far away from Bloomsbury; but it is a smug, urban expanse, and, such as it is, can be reached only by walking along the Euston Road, awfullest of thoroughfares, and is therefore valueless for the purpose of bracing up the spirits of the Bloomsburyites and giving them that lively faith in themselves and in their works which is just what, in my daily rovings around the district, and in my observings of the passers-by, they seemed to me to lack. The passers-by were never many. The inhabitants didn't seem to take much exercise. They seemed to be mostly at home and at work all day. And it may be that none of the young men and women who passed by me was a poet or a painter, or even a critic. But some of them, I thought, must be something of that kind. And I wished they would bear themselves more proudly. I did not demand of them defiance. I merely craved an air of young self-confidence—a pleasant touch of juvenile swagger. Their work was treated with deep respect by most of the elderly reviewers (terrified of not seeming abreast of the times). But they seemed to be not elated by the timorous eulogies that were heaped on them. Their eyes lacked lustre. Their cigarettes drooped almost vertically from between lips that never broke into a smile. And sometimes, I noted, they were wearing very muddy shoes though the sun had for several days been shining brilliantly. But there was one of them (and he is a foreigner, I was told) who stood out distinctly from the rest: he was a tall, thin, keen-faced man with short side-whiskers; and he wore a kind of tam-o'-shanter, a brick-coloured cloak, a long robe to match, and a pair of sandals; and his brown hair fell to the back of his waist, and in windy weather streamed out behind him with immense vivacity. He attracted great attention always, and comment too, of course. The best comment on him that I overheard was made by one of two costermongers whom he had just passed by. "Well, Bill," said the one to the other, who was grinning widely, "at any rate 'e's got more courage than wot *we've* got."

These words, so typical of Cockney wisdom and tolerance, impressed me deeply. And perhaps it was they that caused me, me too, to become courageous. I had read in letters to the Press many hostile references to "the Old School Tie," as a symbol of snobbish devotion to an individuality-crushing old horrid system, and had thought to myself, "What nonsense!" It had never occurred to me to exercise my right to wear such a tie. But now, here, in the heart of Bloomsbury, I felt that I would belatedly do so, and I went to my hosier and ordered two Old Carthusian ties. Do you know the colours? They are three: bright crimson, salmon pink, and royal blue. They are dangerous to the appearance of even a quite young man. To that of an old man they are utterly disastrous. Nevertheless, I, without faltering, wore one of my pair until my sojourn in Bloomsbury came to its end.

This was in October 1936. The Anglo-Italian horizon had cleared. I returned to my home in Italy. In August of the next year but one, that horizon was again dark. One didn't know at what moment Hitler might strike, nor whether Mussolini wouldn't strike with him. Behold me again upon this isle!—but, this time, in Bayswater, where, indeed, I had been born and had lived (barring schoolterms) until I was sixteen. A touching picture. The return of the old native.

There, in Inverness Terrace, I abode for some months, remembering Bloomsbury, and marvelling how two districts with but a few miles between them could have inhabitants so immeasurably different.

Bayswater! Is there no magic for you, reader, in that name? There had been none in it for me. But I'm not at all sure that it won't be found graven on my heart— graven there by the feeble hand of Bloomsbury.

Is it the climate that makes the difference? Bayswater is on a higher level, certainly. Or is it the soil? Bloomsbury, I am sure, is on clay, and Bayswater on gravel. Or is it the presence of Kensington Gardens? As is the river to

Chelsea, so is (or are?) Kensington Gardens to Bayswater—exhilarating, purging, cobweb-preventing, spirit-
of-village-preserving. Even in the darkest days of the au-
tumnal crisis the mien of the inhabitants was suggestive
of Merrie England. Swinging was their gait, bright were
their eyes, clear their complexions, obviously high their
spirits. The scene was Arcadian, the scene seemed vernal.
The young women hadn't masked their faces with make-
up nor plucked out their eyebrows, and weren't smoking,
and were mostly wheeling perambulators with babies in
them. The young men accompanying them seemed not to
have a care in the world, and were mostly wearing Old
School Ties. And the old people looked quite young.
Time does not age the people of Bayswater.

1940

OLD CARTHUSIAN MEMORIES

I AM AFRAID I was never an Old Carthusian of the straitest sect. I remember that in my first term at Oxford (A.D. 1890) I did a drawing of Thomas Sutton, whose features had been so familiar to me during the past five years; and under it I wrote these three elegiac couplets:

FLORUIT innumeros Schola Carthusiana per annos,
  Olim Londinii pessima pernicies.
FLORET in aerio jam condita vertice montis
  Quingentosque docet tristitiam pueros.
FLOREBIT, nec non Plutonis regna manebunt.
  Altera ut agnoscam sum memor alterius.

The drawing was a gross caricature of that grand old merchant, and the verses were an unpardonable libel on my views. I thought Charterhouse a very fine school really. I was very glad of having been there. But—no, I was *not* of the straitest sect. My delight in having been at Charterhouse was far greater than had been my delight in being there. I was well content to be where I was: in Oxford. I am well content to be where I am: in Rapallo. The straitest sect is never happy. It simply can't bear the thought of having left Charterhouse. After-life for it is one long anticlimax. It simply can't forget that goal which Gownboys kicked in that match against Hodgsonites. It cherishes all the old jokes about Monsieur Petilleau. It remembers how prismatically in winter-time the morning sun used to glow through the east window of Chapel. It would gladly be liable to write out and show up a hundred lines or more for whatever fault it may commit. It recalls how splendidly Prescott mi. scored off old Judson about those decimals. It still vibrates with the thrill it felt on that Saturday evening when the Rifle Corps brought back the Ashburton Shield from Bisley for the fourth time running. The future leaves it cold. The present enchants it not at all. It sees even now the black eye that Simpson gave Thompson for calling him a rotter. And it dies with the word *Adsum* on its lips.

"*C'est bien beau, cet amour qui est plus fort que la mort.*" But is it not rather hard on a man's wife and children and friends? *Ought* he to walk backwards along the high-road of life, with his eyes ever yearningly fixed on the more and more distant spires of his old school? Carthusiana Domus—a beautiful phrase, yes. Let a boy at school regard his school as a home, if he can do so, by all means. But let him not be homesick for it ever after. I said that I was "afraid" I did not belong to the straitest sect. That was not quite sincere. It was but an orator's device for conciliating his audience at the outset. I am very glad not to be of the straitest sect, and glad also that this sect is not (so far as I have been able to observe) a large one. Passionately retroverted Old Etonians are common enough in my experience; and I have known a great number of quite maudlin Old Wykehamists. But among Old Carthusians I have noted few cases of schoolsickness (that terrible scourge) in its more virulent forms. Perhaps the keenly bracing air of the Surrey hilltop tends to destroy in a lad's breast the germs of excessive sentiment. If Dr. Haig-Brown had been an ordinary, conservative, unimaginative man, saying, "All's for the best in this best of all possible Greyfriars," and had *not* led his flock forth (in 1872, wasn't it?) to those pastures above Godalming, perhaps we Old Carthusians would be less sanely romantic than we are. Climate does much. Architecture also, I think, does something. Charterhouse is very handsome. This epithet is not one which would leap to the lips of a man beholding Eton or Winchester—or Charterhouse in the City of London. Of such places no man would say, "How well-adapted to the purpose in view! The very stones cry out 'Efficiency'!" Those mouldering stones and discoloured bricks, all that decaying wood-work, strike no chord in the practical side of our nature. They do not seem anxious to satisfy us. They seem to be brooding over old memories. And we find ourselves brooding with them. Had Thomas Sutton had a roving eye and adventurous spirit, like Dr. Haig-Brown, and seen yonder hilltop, and climbed it, and said to his stonemasons, "It is here that ye shall build," then, I fancy again, there might be less sanity than there is in our Old Carthusian romanticism. I never see Charterhouse without reflecting how good for me were the five years I spent there. But I have not that unreasonable emotion which comes to me when I revisit Oxford. Oxford, too, was good for me, in its different way. Yet I do not think there of any gain I may have had therefrom. The practical side of my nature falls into abeyance. This happens also, to some extent, when I go to Greyfriars. I feel there rather as an American of English ancestry may be supposed to feel when he visits England: "Here is the beautiful little old cradle of my race." But the American has to reflect that he himself was never rocked in that cradle. He knows he has a strong American accent. In Greyfriars I feel that I have a strong Surrey accent, and only a rather remote kinship with Addison and Steele.

The good that those aforesaid five years did me— "isn't," my young readers interrupt me, "very clear to *us*." I was about to say that had I been educated by a private tutor I should have become a prig and an egoist. "But," say my young readers, "isn't that just what you *have* become?" To a certain extent, yes, perhaps. But I should be much worse if I hadn't been at Charterhouse. I am, moreover, much better than my young readers suppose. When the Editor of *The Carthusian* asks one to write some memories, it is difficult to avoid egoism. And I am not really priggish when I haven't a pen in my hand, believe me. The very fact that I foresaw your distaste for what I have written shows that I have a power of getting outside myself. That is a very useful power. And it is a power which a shy and sensitive little boy learns better at a public school than he could anywhere else. A private tutor might have made me proficient in French, in Algebra, even in Science. Of these subjects (partly, but only partly, because I had no natural bent for them) I knew

next to nothing when I left Charterhouse. The main thing
that I had learnt there, and have not yet forgotten, was a
knack of understanding my fellow creatures, of living in
amity with them and not being rubbed the wrong way by
their faults, and not rubbing them the wrong way with
mine. I live in Italy nowadays, because I like the sun very
much. But whenever I go to England my friends are really
pleased to see me. I have not lost that good-humoured
give-and-take spirit which only the communal life of a
public school could have given me. It is often complained
that public schools tend to repress individuality in a child.
Charterhouse in the eighteen-eighties did not at all tend
that way—and doesn't, I am sure, now. Its traditions left
plenty of latitude. I was a queer child. I didn't care a brass
farthing for games. What I liked was Latin prose, Latin
verse, and drawing caricatures. Nobody bothered me to
play games. Boys and masters alike (Mr. Tod always especially) encouraged me to draw as many and as impu-
dent caricatures as possible. I ought to have been very
happy. But—oh, how I always longed to be grown-up!
Boys are mostly not cursed with a strong instinct towards
independence; nor men mostly, for the matter of that. I,
alas, was. My lips duly said *Adsum* for me at the right
moment, on the appointed spot. But my heart was always
out of bounds. There was an old gentleman who used
often to pass in front of the garden of Duckites, driving a
phaeton slowly up the steep road. He wore a square-
topped brown hat, he had an aquiline nose and a droop-
ing white moustache and an air of command, and a groom
behind him. I don't know who he was. But I knew that he
could stay out as long as he liked, and would dress for
dinner, and be dining while I sat in Banco, and be fast

asleep when I was in Chapel next morning. I wished immensely that I were he. But now, after all, I am glad that I had to go on being myself. I rejoice that I was not able to skip even one of the years that were so good for me. And if ever I am born into a second incarnation ("Which Heaven forbid!" say my young readers) I hope I shall be sent back to my old school.

1920

THE TOP HAT

WHAT IS THAT?" the very young will ask; and their
parents, ever quick to correct, will say to them,
"You mean, What *was* it?" For it is, of course, very definitely, a thing of the past; almost a museum piece. Indeed,
some parents, those who are less than middle-aged, may
not even have heard of it. I plead guilty to finding in the
past a charm which the present lacks for me. I hasten to
say, however, that this charm is slight in comparison with
that which the future would have for me if I were youngish, for (I gather from many publicists) the future, the
post-bellum period, is to be perfectly splendid: new men,
new ideas, new policies, new cosmic outlooks, new hills
and valleys, new Old Masters, new fathers and mothers,
new wines, new Old Moore's Almanacs, new everything.
But I, alas, shan't live to see much, or perhaps anything,
of all that. And I fondly strain my time-dimmed eyes

towards that backward horizon whereon stands the top hat, a black but shining old monument.

Just *how* old, I can't say. I do but know that it had been erected already in the later days of Charles James Fox. He wears a top hat in that fine portrait of him sitting in his garden, immensely corpulent, but still full of energy and animation, of benignity and genius. He wears it pushed cheerfully back from his brow, and it looks rather odd in relation to his knee-breeches: a queer blend of the new and the old century. It is a beaver hat, of course. The silken kind was a Victorian discovery. But I think that had I been in that garden when that portrait was in the making I should have been shocked that the sitter was not wearing a gold-laced tricorn; for even in those days I should not have been a great approver of current things. Fox himself, no doubt, was very proud of the new head-gear. Perhaps he himself invented it? Had he not, a few years before, said in writing to a friend about the fall of the Bastille, "How much the greatest thing it is in history! and how much the best!"? Strange that a hat that was to symbolise all that was most static and most reputable may have been designed by a man so dangerous!

I imagine that the Whigs, who in all things followed the beloved Charles like sheep, were soon enthusiastic wearers of the top hat, while the Tories looked on it with frigid horror and would have none of it. But very soon, long before the dreadful Reform Bill, they themselves were wearing it, sullenly perhaps, but without protest. It had imposed itself upon them, with a mysterious and inexorable power that was somehow latent in it. It had ceased to be a sign of the times. It had become a natural phenomenon. It seemed to be even a part of the human body.

Not merely did one hunt in it, as one still does: one fished, one skated, one played cricket in it. One wore it throughout debates in the Houses of Parliament, taking it off (with a wrench) only when one rose to orate, and resuming it (with a sigh of relief) as soon as ever one had said one's say. At routs and receptions, however great the crush, one carried it in one's hand all the time—and one must have been glad when, some time in the 'sixties, somebody invented the crush-hat, the gibus, which could be held under the arm, inobtrusively saving the situation. One kept it on one's head, even while eating luncheon in one's club. I don't think there are any clubs now where this custom survives. But it did survive in quite recent years at the "In and Out," magically wafting any guest into a past age. Until quite lately, in theatres or opera houses, when you went out to smoke in the foyer, you always took your hat with you lest some evil thing should befall you. And when you paid an "afternoon call" (a habit not then extinct) you would rather have died than not appear before your hostess hat in hand—and gloves there too. These things you presently placed upon the floor beside your chair, where she could still see them, symbols of good breeding and reassuring proclamations of the fact that you were only a visitor and hadn't come to abide with her for ever.

On Sundays the top hat acquired an even sacred significance. When a family entered the family pew, the father, instead of kneeling down with his wife and children for some moments, merely sat forward and said his silent prayer into his hat. This always puzzled me. I did not grasp the underlying theory that a prayer offered through that medium was likely to be the more acceptable.

On Sundays at Oxford—I was going to use again the adverb "recently," but though the time when I was a freshman seems to me only yesterday, it is now just half a century ago—there were still some undergraduates who honoured the day with top hats and frock-coats. And no undergraduate who, in defiance of proctorial regulations, dared to pay a flying visit to London, would have dared to do so without those urban insignia, though they invited detection on the way to the railway station. One bespoke a cab on the eve of the adventure, and on the morning of it one instructed the cabman to drive to the station very quickly; and on the platform, if one espied a donnish-looking man, one tried to look very old and irreproachable. A motor-car would have been a great convenience. But motor-cars were not yet. And the top hats which in later days they, as it were, bashed in, and the accompanying frock-coats which, so to speak, they ran over, were still vitally necessary to any young gentleman with any self-respect and respect for London.

Or, for that matter, to any decently modest young gentleman who didn't want to be stared at. In London even the crossing-sweepers mostly wore top hats. The "old-clo'-men," those hoarsely vocal perambulants, went even further: they wore three, one rammed down on another, in token, I suppose, of big business. The policemen had indeed long ago taken to helmets—not, I am sure, of their own accord, but because some Home Secretary had thought they would look more frightening. There was only one other civilian body of men that did not follow the all-prevailing fashion: nearly all the actors wore billicocks. The comedians tended to wear brown ones, the tragedians black ones; and those tragedians who were Bohemian in their way of life were apt to prefer sombreros. The actor-manager attended rehearsals in a top hat; and a top hat could be worn also by any actor who had played leading parts in other theatres, and very careful was such an one to wear it, to the envy of less illustrious members of the cast. I always wished those others would combine to break loose and fly in the face of immemorial etiquette, boldly encylindered. But they never fulfilled my hope. Nowadays, I suppose, not even the most eminent and responsible of actors rehearses in anything but what (heaven knows why) is called a trilby. Alas, the Spirit of the Age is one that levels down, not up.

Bank-messengers, Westminster boys, the porter at either end of such places as the Albany or Palace Gardens Terrace, are faithful among the few. And there is of course the occasional, the spasmodic fidelity of men going to weddings or funerals, or (in peace-time) to Ascot or the Eton and Harrow match. My heart is gladdened at sight of these? At the risk of seeming querulous, I protest that it isn't. The males of the Latin races are far less self-conscious than we, far more adaptable in the matter of costume. Carnival time in any French or Italian city is a very good time indeed. The revellers do revel in their fantastic attire, are urged up by it to the height of high spirits. But among my memories none is drearier than that of the Fancy Dress Balls which used to be given in Covent Garden Opera House. The women seemed happy enough, but the men—how woebegone! how deeply ashamed of themselves! The street acrobats of my childhood, in their spangles and pink tights, acquitted themselves quite gaily throughout their professional somersaults and other feats. But when they finished, when they fared along the pavements to their next pitch, what shuffling figures of embarrassment they did cut, to be sure! Not less awfully abashed by their own appearance are the gentlemen going their way to and from weddings or any other of those functions which involve what has become, quite obviously, fancy dress.

Perhaps after the present war the top hat will never reappear at any function whatsoever, even on the head of the eldest man. Perhaps it will be used as a flower-pot in the home, filled with earth and nourishing the bulb of a hyacinth or other domestic flower. I hope, in the goodness of my heart, the housemaid will not handle it untenderly, and will brush it the right way. For it is very sensitive. Its sensibility was ever one of its great charms. It alone among hats had a sort of soul. If one treated it well, one wasn't sure it didn't love one. It wasn't as expressive as one's dog, yet it had an air of quiet devotion and humble comradeship. It had also, like one's cat, a great dignity of its own. And it was a creature of many moods. On dull cloudy days itself was dull, but when the sun was brightly shining, it became radiant. If it was out in a downpour of rain, without an umbrella, it suffered greatly: it was afflicted with a sort of black and blue rash, most distressing to behold, and had to be nursed back to health with tender and unremitting care. Nature herself was the best nurse, however, during the early stages of the malady. The patient was best left to grow quite dry by action of the air, before being ever so gently brushed with the softest of brushes. Gradually it became convalescent, and seemed to smile up at you while it was rubbed slowly with a piece of silk. And anon it was well enough to be ironed. When I was very young I used to have my hat ironed periodically at my hatter's, like other young men. Rather a fascinating process to watch!—the expert swiftness and sureness of it, the immense change wrought with a violent celerity that seemed dangerous and yet did no harm. But in later times I would not entrust my dumb friend to hireling hands howsoever trustworthy, and he almost spoke his gratitude to me when I purchased an iron of the kind required—or rather two irons, a wide one for shaft and crown, a narrow one for brim—and tentatively ironed him myself. At first my 'prentice hand was slow and faulty, and I never did quite master the art of swirling the curves of the iron with perfect symmetry around the crown. I must confess also that more than once, in the early days, I miscalculated the temperature of the iron and did grievous hurt to my friend—hurt so grievous that though he mutely assured me that it was no matter, and implored me not to abandon him, I had to secure a successor instantly.

But, as I look back across the gulf that lies between me and those Victorian and Edvardian years, I feel that I may justly claim to have deserved the affection my hats had for me. And I hope that my young readers will not scoff—though I fear they will—at the fullness with which that feeling was reciprocated by me.

1940

FENESTRALIA

"THE MOTHER OF SISERA looked out at a window, and cried through the lattice, Why is his chariot so long in coming? Why tarry the wheels of his chariot?"

A vivid scene, this, is it not? You *see* it, *hear* it; and you are moved by its dramatic irony, knowing what the mother does not know; knowing what Jael has done.

"And when Jehu was come to Jezreel, Jezebel heard of it; and she painted her face and tired her head, and looked out at a window. And as Jehu entered in at the gate, she said, Had Zimri peace, who slew his master? And he lifted up his face to the window, and said, Who is on my side? who? And there looked out to him two or three eunuchs."

Some dramatic irony here, too. Jezebel knows not, as do we, how imminent her doom is. But the irony is less poignant, forasmuch as Jezebel is not a sympathetic personage. We cannot, with the best will in the world, feel very sorry for her. Nevertheless, her words haunt us as do those of the mother of Sisera. Thanks, in some measure, to Coverdale, to Tyndale? No doubt. But also because her words were spoken, like those others, from a window.

Had either of those women been seated in a room, or walking in a garden, or looking across a wall, we should be far less impressed. People seen or things said indoors or out-of-doors have not the same arresting quality as things said or people seen half-indoors, half-out. There is much virtue in a window. It is to a human being as a frame is to a painting, as a proscenium to a play, as "form" to literature. It strongly defines its content. It excludes all but what it encloses. It firmly rivets us. In fact, it's a magic casement.

I have set eyes on many great men, in my time, and have had the privilege of being acquainted with some of them (not of knowing them well, understanding them well, for to do that there must be some sort of greatness in oneself). And of all the great men whom I have merely seen the one who impressed me most was Degas. Some forty years ago I was passing, with a friend, through the Place Pigalle; and he, pointing up his stick to a very tall building, pointing up to an open window *au cinquième*— or was it *sixième*?—said, "There's Degas." And there, in the distance, were the head and shoulders of a grey-bearded man in a red béret, leaning across the sill. There Degas was, and behind him, in there, was his studio; and behind him, there in his old age, was his life-work; and with unageing eyes he was, I felt sure, taking notes of the "values" and what-not of the populous scene down below, regretting perhaps (for he had never cast his net wide) the absence of any ballet-dancers, or jockeys, or laundry-girls, or women sponging themselves in hip-baths; but deeply, but passionately observing. There he was, is, and will always be for me, framed.

Not perhaps a great, but certainly a gifted and remarkable man was Dr. Jowett, at first and last sight of whom, driving along the Broad in a landau, more than half a century ago, I, a freshman, experienced a mild thrill. How much less mild must have been the thrill vouchsafed to that party of visitors whom C. S. Calverley was showing over Balliol many years earlier! "There," said Calverley, "is the Jowler's window. And," he added, having picked up a stone and hurled it at the window, "there's the Jowler." It is thus, and thus only, that a man is seen at his best—or, for that matter, a woman at hers. In Robert Browning's great galaxy of women none is so vivid to me as Riccardi's bride, and never have I passed Palazzo Riccardi without wondering whether "The Statue and the Bust" would ever have been written had not Duke Ferdinand's first sight of that bride been framed in one of those windows, that window at which he was evermore content to see her, to leave her, day after day, as he rode by.

She, you will remember, when she was growing old, summoned to her presence Luca della Robbia and bade him mould a portrait of her at her habitual window, so that after her death she would still be there. And perhaps it was her example that in later times set the fashion of those *finte* which were until recent years so frequently to be seen on blank walls of Italian houses. These were not up to the standard of "Robbia's craft so apt and strange." They were indeed, if you will, rather vulgar. The average leaner-out was apt to be somewhat over-dressed in the complex mode of the eighteen-seventies, over-frilled, over-jewelled; and her blond tresses (for, of course, to suit the wistful taste of the Italians, she was always a *biondina*) were rather over-blond. The curtains of her window were of a very bright red or blue, and there was likely to be a very yellow canary in a cage beside her. And hers was a vapid simper as she leaned forth with one elbow on the cushioned sill, and one index finger posed upon her cheek. There was much to be said against her; yet one misses her, now that she's gone. She had the charm of windowhood.

I have often wondered that (barring the artless makers of those *finte*) so few painters have used that charm, woven that spell. Dante Gabriel Rossetti, one of those few, might, with his constant striving after "intensity," have been expected to be a devotee of windows; but even he did but once avail himself of frame within frame. Once; and of all his portraits of women, haunting as these are by reason of what he saw in them, or transfused into them, assuredly the most haunting is that of the head and shoulders of a cottage girl at a small lattice window, a girl in a smock, drawing back a chequered curtain, looking out into the morning, and (one guesses) taking in the scent of the flowers in a small front-garden unseen by us. Behind her, unseen too, is her room, with such little belongings in it as are hers; and, just because it isn't visible, that room is a far better setting then those elaborate environments of wondrous fabrics, of mediaeval bibelots, and of exotic flowers in strange bowls or vases with which Rossetti, for the most part, endowed his models.

A great element in the charm of windows is that unless they are on the ground-floor and you flatten your nose against the panes you cannot see more than a very little, if anything at all, of what lies behind them. Your imagination has free play. Do you know those tiny little old half-length figures in waxwork at Hertford House?—those Spanish noblemen and noblewomen of the seventeenth century, each of them enshrined in a square box that is black outside and black inside and has one side made of glass to allow the inmate to look, sombrely, disdainfully out at us from what our fancy assures us is a great old august apartment in a worthy palace? I have often gazed at them, and never without an illusion of having been wafted back across three centuries into Madrid, or into Seville, and of seeing this and that great personage alive, haughtily in the flesh, at a great window. Henry James, roaming around the Boboli Gardens, some fifty years ago, paused and, gazing fixedly up at one of the windows of the vast stony palace, reflected that from *it* Medici after Medici had stood looking out. "And the Medici were great people," he mused, as he tells us in the essay that he presently wrote; and "the ache of the historic spirit" in him was poignant. He would have experienced no such ache in that room on the ground-floor of Hertford House in which I so often stood before the windows of those minim waxworks. His historic sense would have blest and feasted.

Playwrights, like painters, have been chary of windows. Shakespeare, like Rossetti, used only one, once only, so far as I remember. He seems not to have realised that words spoken from a window are thereby as much the more effective as the person seen thereat. Stage-struck young ladies, by some queer instinct, are aware of this fact; hence the desire of all of them to commence as Juliet: the window will conceal incompetence. My most vivid memory of Mrs. Patrick Campbell is framed in the window of Mélisande. And this memory reminds me that Mélisande's was not the only window vouchsafed to us by Maurice Maeterlinck, and that of all his plays *Intérieur* was the most strangely moving and haunting. The foreground of the stage is a garden in the dusk of night. In the background there are the windows of a lighted room, in which, clearly visible, are the father and mother and sisters of a girl whose drowned body, as we know from the hushed and broken talk of the men and women in the garden, is being brought from the river. The mother and father and sisters will soon know what is known to us. The action of the piece lasts no more than half-an-hour. But at the end of it one seems to have suffered a very long period of pity and awe.

Let me pass on to another play, in itself less remarkable than *Intérieur*, but far more famous and more popular. Its author is nameless, its action is crudely barbarous, its dialogue is but shrill incoherent gibberish. Yet it has for all of us, whenever we come across it, a perennial fascination. How can we account for that? Easily enough. The whole drama is enacted in a window-frame, the frame of the one and only window in Punch's strange old portable house.

Politicians, please note. The gift of oratory has been conferred on few of you; nor are many of you able to express yourselves fluently, accurately, and without grievous triteness. Think how much less restive your audiences would be if you spoke to them through a window! My temperament was conservative even in my youth. My mind, moreover, was ossified years ago. I abominate all alterations. But for your sakes I do hope you will insist that St. Stephen's new Chamber shall have a small inner structure, simple or ornate, with a window through which all speeches shall be delivered. Let me also commend to you a similar device on the platforms of Town Halls. Even that baker's dozen of you who *can* speak with the tongue of men and angels, and can hold their constituents or their fellow Members spellbound, would find their triumphs enhanced by my scheme. I suppose that the greatest English orator in the nineteenth century was Mr. Gladstone; and I take it to have been the peak of his achievements in the spoken word that on a bitterly cold afternoon, and on Blackheath Common, at the time of the Bulgarian Atrocities, he dominated and swayed for one hour and a half a gathering of not less than six thousand persons, most of whom had violently booed him at the outset of his speech. There, indeed, was a man who could dispense with windows. Yet, in later years, in the Midlothian phase of his career, he made frequent use of them. And I feel sure his greatest effects were made in those successive railway stations where, to serried throngs, he spoke burning words from the window of a railway-carriage, on his way northward or southward. I can see that ivory face and that silvery hair; and those dark flashing eyes looking forth. Would that I had been there to hear the organ-music of the voice!

Gladstone's great rival and antithesis was no man for mobs, and excelled only in the Chamber. But he did have one great success in presence of a multitude. I refer to the one and only occasion on which he spoke from a window. I wish I had been old enough to be in the crowd down to which, from a frame on the first floor of 10, Downing Street, he made his pronouncement about Peace

with Honour. I should like also, of course, to have heard
him in parliamentary debate. I was once told by an old
gentleman who had sat on the back benches, as a Conservative member, when Mr. Disraeli was Leader of the
House, that, sphinx-like though the face was to all be-
holders, the great debater's back was very expressive—
the movements of the shoulders, of the elbows and the
hips vividly illustrating his words. But even in repose a
back, if it be of the right kind, can be eloquent—such a
back as Goethe's, for example. Do you know that sketch
which Johann Tischbein made in one of the bedrooms of
a Roman inn, while Goethe was leaning out of the window and looking down to the street below? It is a graceful, a forceful, and a noble back that we see there in that
bedroom. Had Napoleon been there to see it, he would
have murmured, as you know he did when he saw Goethe
face to face at Weimar in later years, *"Voilà un homme!"*
It is moreover the back of a man rapt in contemplation,
rapt in the joy of being, at last, in the city of his dreams;
a man avidly observing, learning, storing up. He is wearing slippers, he has not yet put on his waistcoat nor but-
toned his breeches at the knees. His toilet can wait. His
passionate curiosity cannot. It is as intimate, as significant a portrait as ever was made of one man by another.

I like to think that it may have been made on Goethe's
very first morning in Rome, and that he had arrived over-
night. In visiting a city that you have never yet seen it is
well to arrive at night, for sake of the peculiar excitement of next morning's awakening to it—the queer deep
thrill of your prospection into whatever street or square
underlies your window, presaging all else that will be
seen later. A square is preferable to a street; a populous

old spacious square, set with statues and animated by fountains; somewhere in Italy, for choice. Such a square is a good starting-point for your future rovings; and to it from them you will always return with a feeling of affection, and will spend much time at that window of yours, fondly. But I beg your pardon for dogmatising about you. When I said *you*, I meant *I*. You perhaps are an ardent sight-seer, a scrupulous examiner of aisles and sacristies and side-chapels, an indefatigable turner-in at turnstiles of museums and picture-galleries and the like. I'm an alfrescoist. The life of the city, and the architectural background against which that life is lived, suffice my soul while I rove around, or merely lean forth from the window that is, for the time being, mine. Merely? I take back that word. One is more observant from one's coign of vantage up there, and all that is to be seen stands out more clearly, and one's mind is more sensitive, than when one pads the hoof down there.

"The last time I saw Paris"—otherwise than from the *ceinture* railway—abides with me more vividly and delightfully than any of the previous times. Yet I saw but one aspect of the city's life. You know the huge grey façade of the Gare du Nord, and may have noted that it is adorned (or at any rate weighted) with rows of proportionately huge statues, one on each side of every window, symbolising the continents, and the principal French provinces and cities, and Liberty, I think, and Justice, and many other things of national or universal import. But you may not be aware that all the windows on the first floor are those of an hotel, an hotel that occupies this one floor only, and consists of twelve vast bedrooms (each with a small anteroom and a bathroom), and nothing else.

Behind the bedrooms runs a corridor whose opposite side
has windows through which you see, far down, the many
platforms of the station and the steam of arriving and de-
parting trains. These windows are of thick double glass.
The corridor is a quiet one. Little locomotives are seen
and not heard. But the bedrooms are the great point. They
seem to have been built for giants and giantesses, so vast
are their ancient wardrobes, dressing-tables, and beds;
and each of their two windows is in proportion to the
stone figure that stands on either side of it, planting a
colossal foot upon the sill. If I remember rightly, it was
from between the ankle of a masculine Africa and of a
feminine Marseilles that I looked forth early on my first
morning, and saw a torrent of innumerable young human
backs, flooding across the square beneath and along the
straight wide Rue Lafayette beyond. The fullness and
swiftness of it made me gasp—and kept me gasping, while
in the station behind me, incessantly, for more than an
hour and a half, trainload after trainload of young men
and women from the *banlieue* was disgorged into the capital. The maidens outnumbered the youths by about three
or four to one, it seemed to me; and yet they were one
maiden, so identically alike were they in their cloche hats
and knee-deep skirts and flesh-coloured stockings, and in
virtue of that erectly tripping gait which Paris teaches
while London inculcates an unsteady slouch. One maiden,
yet hundreds and thousands of maidens, each with a soul
of her own, and a home of her own, and earning her own
wages. Bewildering! Having seen that sight, I needed no
other. During the three or four days of my sojourn I
didn't bother to go anywhere, except for meals in a little

restaurant hard by, famous for its oysters and its bouilla-
baisse. I spent my time in reading newspapers and books,
and in looking forward to the early morrow's renewal of
the incalculable torrent.

From some windows one can gaze and be rapt at any
hour of the day, even though no human being is to be
seen from them. From any window, for instance, that
looks out on to the sea. For many years I lived in a little
house that looks down to what a great poet, reared beside
Northumbrian breakers, rudely called "the tideless dolor-
ous midland sea." It has a tide really (though not perhaps
a very great one), and its aspect is constantly changing,
and I was never tired of watching it and its moods. I remember, too, with affection, the little bedroom in an old
farm-house at Pagham, where I abode for some weeks of
the autumn after the last war. There were a few stairs up
to the bedroom, but the window was so placed that its sill
was no more than five feet or so above the level of the
ground. Outside there was nothing to be seen but a large
field of ripening barley. The sea was quite near, but invisible. One was all alone with the barley, which grew in a
friendly eager manner right up against the wall of the
farm-house, inviting one to lean down and touch its ears.

Let not such memories imply any disparagement of
quite ordinary windows—street windows, with recurrent
glimpses of neighbours opposite. I am glad that from the
windows of my nursery in a Victorian cul-de-sac I knew
by sight various other children, and their nurses, and their
parents. I had no great desire to know them outside their
frames. I think I had a shrewd suspicion that they were
not really so interesting and so exciting as my fancy made

them. In my adolescence no neighbours were to be seen. Nevertheless, I was fond of my bedroom window, from which I could gaze in a moralising manner over the multitude of tombstones in what had been throughout the eighteenth century the burial-ground of St. George's, Hanover Square; and I was still fonder of my sitting-room window, from which I could watch, year after year, the budding of the leaves in Hyde Park, and their prime, and their decline and fall. Trees are of course the best thing Nature has to show us; and in London one values them far more than one does elsewhere. I missed them sorely when, in later years, I lived in a street again. The faces at the windows over the way were unchanging, were unaffected by the sequence of the seasons. Also, alas, my talent for weaving fancies was not what it once had been. Still, I was a frequent looker-forth—especially on Thursdays. I had become a professional writer. I wrote a weekly article for *The Saturday Review*; and Thursday was the day on which I did it; and the doing was never so easy as I sometimes hoped it might be: I had never, poor wretch, acquired one scrap of professional facility. I often doubted whether I had in my mind enough to fill the two columns that were expected of me. I sometimes found that I had got ahead of my argument, or even that I was flatly contradicting something that I had said at the outset, or that my meaning was obscure even to myself. At such crises I would rise from my desk and take, as it were, refuge at the window, with brows knitted, and chin tightly clasped between finger and thumb. I would envy the hansom cabmen as they flashed by below me. I would envy some old lady leading a dog on a leash. I would envy her dog.

"And if it was thus, thus in the prime of me," need I say that the composition of what you have just been reading or skipping was not done without much recourse to a window?

1944

T. FENNING DODWORTH

THIS NAME IS SELDOM, if ever, on the lips of the man in the street. But it is a name highly esteemed by men whose good opinion is most worth having. When the idols of our market-place shall have been jerked from their pedestals by irreverent Time, Fenning Dodworth will not be utterly forgotten. His name will crop up *passim*, and honourably, in the pages of whatever Grevilles and Creeveys we have had among us during the past thirty years.— "Met Fenning Dodworth in Pall Mall this morning. He told me he had it on the best authority that St. John Brodrick would not be put up to speak on the Second Reading."—"Heard an amusing and characteristic *mot* of Fenning Dodworth's. He was dining with some other men at E. Beckett's one night last week, when the conversation turned on Winston's speech at Oldham. Beckett said, 'Whatever Winston's faults may be, he has genius.' 'That,' said Dodworth, in the silence that ensued, 'is a proposition on which I should like to meditate before endorsing it.' Collapse of Beckett!"—"Sat next to Dodworth at the Cordwainers' dinner. He said that he did not at all like the look of things in the Far East. Later in the evening I asked him point-blank whether the phrase 'A Government of Pecksniffs,' which has been going the rounds, had been coined by him. 'It may have been,' he said drily. Characteristic!"

Dodworth's wit is undeniable. It is not, certainly, of the kind that I like best and rate highest—the kind that pierces without leaving a wound. Dodworth's shafts are barbed, and, though it were too much to say that they are poisoned, assuredly they have been dipped in very caustic acids. And he has not humour. At least, if he has, he uses it sparingly, and never at all in my presence. But humour, delightful though it is for current purposes, lacks durability. There are fashions in humour, and they are always changing. Wit, on the other hand, being a hard and clean-cut thing, is always as good as new. Dodworth's gems, set in the golden tissues of private journals given to the world, will have lost nothing of their flash. And among readers of those journals there will be a great desire to know what Dodworth himself was like. Keepers of journals are so apt to omit that sort of thing. What faces, complexions, girths, heights, gaits, voices, gestures, tricks of manner, shirt-studs, preferences in food and wine, had the more or less eminent men who were for ever pouring into the diarist's ear their hopeful or fearful conjectures about tomorrow night's Division? The diarist knew, and had therefore no need to tell himself. But *we* don't know, and we want to know. That Division was a turning-point in the world's history? No doubt. Those more or less eminent men are dust? Alas, yes. But they were flesh and blood to the diarist, and he could have made them so to us, too. It may be that the diarists of our own day have held in mind the omissions of their forerunners, and make a point of telling themselves just the things that are a matter of course to them. But it may be otherwise. So I insert here, for posterity, a note or two on the surface of Fenning Dodworth—who, quite apart from his wit, seems to me one of the most remarkable, the strongest and, in a way, most successful men of our time.

Dignity, a Roman dignity, is the keynote of his appearance. This is undoubtedly one of the causes of his success. Is it also, I sometimes ask myself, partly a result of his success? But no. Twenty years ago (when first I made his acquaintance) he was as impressive as he is, at the age of sixty, now. Moreover, had his mind any knack to remould his body, surely he would be taller. He remains very far below the middle height. But he carries his head high, thus envisaging the more easily the ruck of common objects, and making on such of these objects as are animate the kind of effect which his unaided stature might preclude. One of his eyebrows is slightly raised; the other is slightly lowered, to hold in position a black-rimmed single eyeglass. His nose is magnificently Roman. His lips are small, firm, admirably chiselled, and every word that falls from them is very precisely articulated. His chin is very strong, and his chest (in proportion to his height) deep. He has the neatest of hands and feet. Draped in a toga, and without his monocle, he might pass for a statuette of Seneca. But he prefers and affects a more recent style of costume—the style, somewhat, of the Victorian statesmen who flourished in his youth: a frock-coat and a rather large top hat, a collar well open at the throat, and around it a riband of black silk tied in a loose bow. He is a good judge (and, I take it, the sole survivor among judges) of sherry. Nor is this the only way in which he imparts agreeably the flavour of a past age. In Thackeray, in Trollope, in the old volumes of *Punch*, you will have found a wealth of testimony to the fact that persons of high importance, meeting persons of slight importance, often did not shake hands, but offered a finger or two to be shaken. Incredible, nevertheless? Then perhaps you will not believe me when I say that I have been offered two fingers by Dodworth. Indignantly you ask whether I shook them. I avoid your eye, I evade your question, I do but say that I am very susceptible to—well, to greatness.

The proof, for me, of Dodworth's greatness is in what he has achieved. He has made so much out of so little. Many men have been ten times more successful (in the coarse sense of that word) without winning a tithe of what he has won. It is often said that nothing succeeds like success. Dodworth's career offers a corrective of such cynicism—or would do so if his case were a common one. I admit that to have excelled in some undertaking is not always needed for the making of a great prestige. Dukes and princes are not without honour even if they have done nothing—or even if they shall have tried to do something and failed. Dodworth was not born exempt from the advisability of doing something. "*b*. 12 Feb. 1860, *o.s.* of J. Dodworth and Rachel, *e.d.* of W. K. Fenning, of Norwich." Thus does he speak, in *Who's Who*, of his origin; and as he is (albeit less a toady than any man I know) one of the most finished snobs I have ever met, his reticence tells much. Old Mr. Dodworth was of some town so mean that it is not mentionable. And what did he do there?

What, for that matter, did old Mr. Fenning do at Norwich? Something dreadful, you may be sure, from the social standpoint. What school was the young Dodworth sent to? Obviously to some school, else we should find "*Educ*: privately." There is no mention of any school. The boy went to some school that is unmentionable. But it may be surmised that he did well there, for we do find "*Educ*: Won open scholarship at Queen's Coll., Oxford, 1879." A presage, this, of coarse successes. But mark the sequel! "Second Class in Classical Mods., 1881; Third Class, Lit. Hum., 1883. Treasurer of Union, 1882." He was thrice a candidate for the Presidency of the Union; and I happen to have met in later years two of his successful opponents, both of them men rather prominent in public life today. One of them told me that Dodworth's speeches were the wittiest ever heard in the Union "or, I do believe, anywhere else"; the other described them as the most closely reasoned. And neither of these men spoke of Fenning Dodworth as one who had not lived up to his early promise. They seemed to pride themselves, rather, on having always foreseen his ascendancy.

Men prominent in public life are mostly hard to converse with. They lack small-talk, and at the same time one doesn't like to confront them with their own great themes. I have found that the best way to put them at their ease, to make them expand and glow, is to mention Fenning Dodworth. They are all, from their various standpoints, of one mind about him. Judges think he would have been an ornament to the Bench, statesmen wish he were in the Cabinet, diplomatists wish he were one of them, and wish he could be at Tokyo or Pekin or wherever at the moment his grasp of things in the Far East and his unfailing

dislike of the look of them would be most obviously inval-
uable. And all these gods console themselves with anecdotes of his wit—some mordant thing he said years ago,
some equally mordant thing he said last week. "I remember," a Judge will tell you, "one night at mess on the
Northern Circuit, somebody said 'I call Bosanquet a very
strong man in Nisi Prius.' Dodworth looked at him in that
queer dry way of his, and said 'Ah! I should hardly go so
far as that.' " The Judge will then throw himself back in
his chair and alarm you with symptoms of choking. If
you ask him why Dodworth did not remain at the Bar, the
answer will be that he got so few briefs: "He was the best
all-round Junior I ever heard, but he wasn't a man for the
jury: you can't saw a plank of wood with a razor. Pity he
didn't practise in Chancery! But I suppose he was right to
devote himself to politics. He's had more scope there."

He has not, certainly, been cramped. For him there has
been no durance within the four walls of the House of
Commons. He contested (I quote again his narrative in
Who's Who) "East Grinstead, 1888; Dulwich, 1890;
Skipton, 1891; Cannock, 1893; Haggerston, 1897; Pon-
typool, 1898; Peebles, 1900." He escaped, every time, the
evils of election. (And his good angel stood not less close
to him on the three occasions when he offered himself as
candidate for the London County Council.) Voters, like
jurors, would not rise to him. At length it was borne in
even on the leaders of his party that they must after all be
content to rely on his pen rather than on his tongue. "Has
been," he says in *Who's Who*, "for many years a contribu-
tor to the leading reviews." That is so. Those reviews are
not edited by the vulgar. Dodworth's MSS. have always
been printed. I used to read articles by him when I was yet

a school-boy, and to wonder whether the Liberal Party would ever again hold up its hideous head. I remember one entitled "The Franchise Bill—And After," and another entitled "The Home Rule Peril—And After." Both seemed to me splendid, partly perhaps because of their titles. Dodworth was, I believe, the first publicist to use that magical affix, that somehow statesmanlike, mysterious, intriguing formula, "—And After." In later years I began to think him narrow in his views. I became a prey to that sentimentalism from which in one's schooldays one is immune, and ceased to regard the ideas of the Liberal Party as perverse. Dodworth as a political thinker seemed to me lacking in generosity, lacking even (despite his invariable "—And After") in foresight. But the older I grew, and the less capable of his doctrine, the more surely did I appreciate his command of literary form. Losing the taste which undergraduates have for conceits and florid graces, I rendered justice to the sombre astringency of Dodworth's prose. Whatever his theme, whatever the Liberal Party was in office proposing, or in opposition opposing, his article was substantially the same as every other article he had written; but, like some masterpiece in music, it never palled. With perfect sobriety and fairness he would state the arguments on which the Liberal spokesmen had been basing their case; he would make these *seem* quite unanswerable; but then, suddenly, like a panther crouching to spring, he would pause, he would begin a new paragraph: "What are the facts?" The panther had sprung. It was always a great moment. I usually skipped the forthcoming facts and went on to the point where Dodworth worked back to first principles and historic parallels and (best of all) quotations from the mighty dead. He was always very adept in what may be called the suspensive method of quotation. "It was written long ago, by one who saw further and grasped more firmly than is given to most men to see and to grasp, that 'the fate of nations is in the conscience of their rulers.' It is for us to ask ourselves whether, in saying this, Mr. Burke was right." Or, "In a speech delivered in the Guildhall at a time when Europe stood in the shadow of great events, a First Minister of the Crown, as to whom not a few of us are agreed in wishing that he were alive today, said that the art of government lay in the construction of safeguards. Mr. Disraeli never spoke a truer word." But presently, with a swoop from the past to the present, and from the general to the particular, the scholar would be merged in the panther, and the Liberal Party be mauled so frightfully that at last even the panther seemed to recoil in pity for "a Party once great" and to wonder if some excuse could not be found for it. The excuse, the last sentence of Dodworth's article, was usually *Quos deus vult perdere prius dementat;* but sometimes, more simply and poignantly, *Quos deus vult.*

Fifteen years ago it seemed to the leaders of his party and to the veiled prophets in their central office that such a voice as his, if it were heard daily by a vast public, would be proportionately more potent than in its monthly addresses to the few. There was an old-established daily newspaper whose proprietor had just died, and his estate not yet been wound up. And there was, on one of the back benches of the party, a stout, silent man, middle-aged, very affluent, a Mister. Some word in season, some word in the ear, was spoken to this man on a moonless night, by one of the veiled prophets. That old-established newspaper was acquired. Dodworth was installed in the editorial chair, gave the key-note to the staff, and wrote every night a leading article with his own incisive pen. But "you cannot," as the Judge said, "saw a plank of wood with a razor." To uneducated readers the almost-daily-recurring phrase *Quos deus vult* had no meaning. Half-educated readers thought it meant "The Lord watch between thee and me when we are absent one from another." The circulation fell by leaps and bounds. Advertisers withdrew their advertisements. Within six months (for the proprietor was now a Sir, and oafishly did not want to become something better) that old-established newspaper ceased utterly to be. "This," I thought, "really *is* a set-back for Dodworth." I was far from right. The set-back was rather for myself. I received no payment for three or four of the book-reviews that I had contributed, and I paid two guineas for my share of the dinner offered to Dodworth at the Savoy Hotel, and five guineas towards a portrait of him "in oils" by one of the oldest and worst of Royal Academicians. This portrait was presented to him after dinner by our chairman (the Prime Minister of that time) in a speech that would have been cloying if it had been more fluent. Dodworth bandied no compliments. This was a private occasion, and he lived up to his reputation of being privately as caustic about his friends as he was publicly about his foes. He "twitted" his friend the Prime Minister with one thing and another, reducing that statesman and the whole company to paroxysms of appreciation. . . . "Our chairman has said that he will continue to do what in him lies to help the cause that we all have at heart [hear, hear]. Well, wherever there is a cause there is also an effect [laughter]. I hope that the effect in this instance will be of the kind that we all desiderate [much laughter]. I do not say that it will be, I only say I hope that it will be [hysterics]." I wish I could recall more of what Dodworth said. Every one agreed that he was in his best vein and had never been more pungent.

Two or three years later I attended another banquet at which he was the guest of the evening—a banquet at the Hotel Cecil, offered by the Playgoers' Club. He had written a three-act comedy: *The Antagonists—A Satire on Certain Aspects of Political Life*. This had been instantly snapped up, and soon produced, with a very strong cast, by Sir George Alexander. All the leaders of both parties in both Houses were present on the first night, and many of them (rashly, so weak were they with laughter) were present also on the second, third, and fourth nights, and would probably have been present on other nights, too; but (such was the absenteeism of the vulgar) there were no other nights. Dodworth had again not sawn the plank. But it was clear to me, a week later, on the Sunday evening fixed—some time previously—for the banquet, that the edge of his razor was quite unblunted. In responding to the speech of the President (who had said nothing to imply that the play was not still running), Dodworth taunted us, very tartly, with our failure to arrest the decay of dramatic art by elevating the taste of the public. Had he been less witty, he might rather have spoilt our evening, so deep did he plant in us a sense of our failure. His own peculiar strength was never better attested than when, later in the evening, Alexander rose and announced with pride that he had that morning secured from his friend Fenning Dodworth the promise to write another comedy for the St. James's Theatre.

As this was never performed, I am quite sure it was never written. And I think the cause of the unfulfillment is to be found in the history of our time. Politics had now become too tense and terrible for the lighter use of Dodworth's pen. After the death of Sir Henry Campbell-Bannerman "a Party once great" cast off what old remnants of decency had clung to it. Mr. Lloyd George composed a Budget. The Lords rejected it. Mr. Asquith introduced the Parliament Bill. Those were stirring times; and during them, as it seemed to me, Dodworth was greater, aye! and happier, than he had ever been. Constitutional points and precedents had always lain very near to his heart. In them he had always both publicly and privately abounded. His dislike of the look of things in the Far East had never been more than skin-deep. Such themes as the Reform Bill of 1832 had ever touched him to far finer issues. The fiscal problems raised by Mr. Chamberlain, strongly though he had backed Mr. Chamberlain's solution of them, had left in abeyance what was best in him. The desirability of enriching some rich manufacturers cannot be expressed in the grand manner. Mr. Asquith's desire to limit the Lords' veto was a worthy theme. Month followed month. I soon lost count of Dodworth's articles. "The Assault on the Constitution—And After," "The Betrayal—And After," "The End of All Things—And After," are the only three that I recall. Enough that he was at his best in all of them, and ended every one of them with the inference that Mr. Asquith (one of his staunchest though most reluctant admirers) was mad.

I had the good fortune to meet him constantly in those days of crisis. I hardly know how this was. I did not seek him out. It seemed simply that he had become ubiquitous. Maybe his zest had multiplied him by 100 or so, enabling him to be in as many places at once. He looked younger. He talked more quickly than was his wont, though with an elocution as impeccable as ever. He had none of those austere, prim silences for which he was so feared. He was a bard. His command of the nobler, the statesmanlike kind of slang, and his unction in the use of it, had never been so mesmeric. "If the Sovereign sent for the P.M. and said 'I shall do nothing till the case arises,' what could the P.M. say? Nothing. On the other hand, if the P.M. sought audience tomorrow *with a view to a contingent assurance,* and the Sovereign said 'That's all very well, but what d'you hypothecate?' and the P.M. simply referred him back to what Mr. G. said when The Buffalo was threatening to throw out the Franchise of '85—*then* what? The Sovereign would be in a damned ticklish position. And the only way out of it" . . . etc. Little wonder that agéd ears played truant at his tales, and younger hearings were quite ravishéd, so sweet and voluble was his discourse.

Alas, the Sovereign did not slip through whatever loophole it was that Dodworth descried. The P.M. did not climb down. The Buffalo did not rise from the grave. Lord L. sold the pass. The backwoodsmen went back to the back-woods. Dodworth was left sitting among the ruins of the Constitution. But the position suited him. He was still in his element, and great. It was at the outbreak of the War that I feared there might be no more of him. And there was, indeed, less. No longer young, he did not acquire more than a smattering of the military idiom, nor any complete grasp of strategy. But he was ever in close touch with the War Office and with G.H.Q., and was still

fairly oracular. Several times in the last year of the conflict, he visited (with temporary rank of Lieutenant-Colo-
nel) certain sectors of the Western Front and made
speeches to the men in the trenches, declaring himself
well satisfied with their *morale,* and being very caustic
about the enemy; but it may be doubted whether he,
whose spell had never worked on the man in the street,
was fully relished by the men in the trenches. *Non omni
omnia.* Colonel Dodworth was formed for successes of
the more exquisite kind. I think the Ministry of Informa-
tion erred in supposing that his article, "Pax Britannica—
And After," would be of immense use all the world over.
But the error was a generous one. The article was translated into thirty-seven foreign languages and fifty-eight
foreign dialects. Twelve million copies of it were printed
on hand-woven paper, and these were despatched in a series of special trains to a southern port. The Admiralty,
at the last moment, could not supply transport for them,
and the local authorities complained of them that they
blocked the dock. The matter was referred to the Ministry of Reconstruction, which purchased a wheat-field
twenty miles inland and erected on it a large shed of con-
crete and steel for the reception of Dodworth's pamphlets,
pending distribution. This shed was nearly finished at the
moment when the Armistice was signed, and it was finished soon after. Whether the pamphlets are in it, or just
where they are, I do not know. Blame whom you will. I
care not. Dodworth had even in the War another of his
exquisite successes.

Yet I am glad for him that we have Peace. At first I was
afraid it might be bad for him. We had been promised a
new world; and to that, though he had come so well

through the War, I feared he would not be able to adjust himself. The new world was to be, in many respects, rather dreadful—a benign cataclysm, but still a cataclysm, and Dodworth perhaps not to be found in any of his favourite chairs when the crystal waters subsided and the smiling land was revealed. We may have it yet. But the danger seems to be less imminent. A few days ago I met Dodworth in Bird-Cage Walk, and said to him something about it seeming likely that moderate counsels would prevail among the Labour men. "Ah," he said in that queer dry way of his, "it's their moderate intelligence that's the danger." He said it instantly (and it was obviously not a thing he could have prepared). And the very fact that he was able to jest once more was a heartening proof for me of his belief that the worst was past. Another good sign was that he had resumed his top hat. During the last eighteen months of the War he had worn a thing of soft black felt, which I took to be a symbol of inward pessimism; and he had gone on wearing this long after the treaty of Peace was signed—a retention which seemed to me equally sinister, as a silent manifesto of unfaith in the future of our body politic. But now he was crowned once more with a cylinder from his old Victorian block. And a further good sign was that he was on his way to the House. In the old days, he had been wont to occupy, whenever an important debate was afoot, one or another of those nice seats near the Serjeant-at-Arms. In the course of the War he had ceased from such attendance. He had become very bitter against "the politicians" and especially "the lawyer politicians." But I suspect that what revolted him even more was the sight of the new, the "business" types on the Treasury Bench—the bullet-headed men in reefer-jackets, rising to tell the House what they were "out for" and what they were "up against," and why they had "pushed" this and "turned down" that, and forgetting to address the Chair. Dodworth's return to St. Stephen's implied for me the obsolescence of such men. I asked him what he thought, from a tactical standpoint, of the line recently taken by the Independent Liberals. "I am afraid," he said, "there is not much hope for these Adullamites without a Cave." This phrase he may not have coined on the spur of the moment. But, even so, how extraordinarily good! It's wicked, it's unjust, it hurts, but—it seems to me even more delicious than his description of Gladstone in '86 as "a Moses without a Pisgah." I think he was pleased, in his queer dry way, by my delight, for he said he would send me a copy of his forthcoming book—a selection from the political articles written by him since his earliest days. He had not, he said (quoting, I think, from his preface), intended to resuscitate these ephemerae. The idea was not his but ——'s (he named the head of an historic firm of publishers). The book will be out next month, and will include that most recent of his articles, "A Short Shrift for Sinn Fein—And After." It will be "remaindered," of course, in a year or so, but will meanwhile have taken an honoured place in every eminent man's library. By the way, I had feared that Mr. Lloyd George, with his Celtic rather than classic mind, made a break in the long line of Prime Ministers who have rated Dodworth highly. I am glad to hear that at a dinner held somewhere the night before last he impulsively rose and proposed Dodworth's health, recalling that when he himself was a bare-legged, wild-eyed, dreamy little lad on the Welsh mountains he read every word of Fenning Dodworth's earlier articles as they came out, and had never forgotten them (applause). Since those days he had met Dodworth many a time in the valley and got some resounding whacks (laughter). But he always felt, and more than ever he felt tonight, that Dodworth and he were destined to walk hand in hand on the heights, misty though those heights might be now, and hail together the glory of the sunrise that, sooner or later, had got to come (prolonged applause). My informant tells me that of all the eyes around the table Dodworth's alone were dry, and maintains that in returning thanks he ought not to have been pungent. I disagree. I want no sign of weakness in dear old Dodworth.

Dear old Dodworth? Well, no—and yet *yes,* too. I don't like him, perhaps; but there is no man whom I so delight to see, to watch, and to think of. I hope he will not predecease me. Of one thing I am sure: he will die game, and his last words will be "—And After?" and will be spoken pungently. And of another thing I am sure; the eminent men of all kinds will sign a petition about him to the Dean of Westminster. But there is a tradition of Philistinism in that Deanery. The voices of the eminent fall on deaf ears there, and only the roar of the man in the street is heard. Dodworth will, characteristically, not have the coarse success of lying in our Abbey. His monument will be found—piecemeal, indeed, but great, but glittering— in the diaries which I mentioned at the outset of this little essay in his honour.

1922

LYTTON STRACHEY

ONE DAY in the springtime of 1912—a date not long ago in point of time, but infinitely long ago in point of the changes that Europe has suffered since then—I was lunching at the Savile Club. I had been living for two years in Italy; and there were some faces new to me. There was one that interested me very much; an emaciated face of ivory whiteness, above a long square-cut auburn beard, and below a head of very long sleek dark-brown hair. The nose was nothing if not aquiline, and Nature had chiselled it with great delicacy. The eyes, behind a pair of gold-rimmed spectacles, eyes of an inquirer and a cogitator, were large and brown and luminous. The man to whom they belonged must, I judged, though he sat stooping low down over his table, be extremely tall. He wore a jacket of brown velveteen, a soft shirt, and a dark red tie. I greatly wondered who he was. He looked rather like one of the Twelve Apostles, and I de-

cided that he resembled especially the doubting one,
Thomas, who was also called Didymus. I learned from a
friend who came in and joined me at my table that he
was one of the Stracheys: Lytton Strachey; a Cambridge
man; rather an authority on French literature; had written a book on French literature in some series or other;
book said to be very good. "But why," my friend asked,
"should he dress like that?" Well, we members of the
Savile, Civil Servants, men of letters, clergymen, scien-
tists, doctors, and so on, were clad respectably, passably,
decently, but no more than that. And "Hang it all," I
said, "why *shouldn't* he dress like that? He's the best-
dressed man in the room!"

Soon afterwards I returned to Italy, and his image
faded from my mind. Two years later I was back in England, but did not again see him, and his image remained
in abeyance. But it instantly and vividly recurred to me
when, in 1917, I was told by Desmond MacCarthy that
a friend of his, Lytton Strachey, was writing a book about
some of the Victorians; that these rather horrified the
author, but that the book was sure to be a good one; and
that I, though I didn't share the horror, would be sure to
like it. A few months later I had the pleasure of meeting
this man at dinner in the house of a gifted lady; and
though I had no separate dialogue with him in the course
of the meal, and though he seemed shy of general conversation, I was impressed by his mild dignity and benign
good manners. Early in the following spring Desmond's
prophecy that I would like the book was more than fulfilled.

I did far more than like it, I rejoiced in it. I can, if you
will let me, lay claim to one little modest negative virtue.

I have always been free from envy. In the year 1900 I had been considered a rather clever and amusing young man, but I felt no pang whatsoever at finding myself cut out at my own game by a sudden newcomer, named G. K. Chesterton, who was obviously far more amusing than I, and obviously a man of genius into the bargain. In 1918 I was young no longer, and I think I amused people less than I had. I had subsided into sober irony. Well, here was an ironist of an order far superior to mine. And here was a delicately effulgent master, a perfect master, of English prose. And in my joy there lurked no asp of satisfaction that here was not, in my opinion, a man of genius. Very exquisite literary artists seldom are men of genius. Genius tends to be careless in its strength. Genius is, by the nature of it, always in rather a hurry. Genius can't be bothered about perfection. Each of the four essays in *Eminent Victorians* was, as a work of art, perfect.

I ventured to send, I could not forbear to send, to Mr. Strachey a reasoned letter of thanks and congratulations, by which he seemed to be pleased. But it was not until the spring of 1921 that I saw him again. I had reverted to Italy soon after the Armistice, and when he mentioned to me in a letter that he was engaged upon the theme of Queen Victoria, I immediately drew—for this time his image had not lapsed from my mind's eye—a caricature of him in his royal connexion. This drawing, with others of other people, I presently brought with me to England, for exhibition; but I wished to verify Strachey's image, and wrote to tell him so, and he was so good-natured as to call on me at my hotel in order that I might professionally stare at him. He was no longer velveteen-jacketed, he was dressed now in a worldlier manner, which, I told him, seemed to me less characteristic, and he willingly agreed that he should remain velveteen-jacketed in my drawing. A few days later, his mother invited me to luncheon. She was old and almost blind, but immensely vivacious, and a very fount of wit, and with her I felt as though I were in the presence of Mme du Deffand; and I knew very surely from whom her son derived some, at least, of the quality of his work.

Thenceforward, whenever I was in London, I met him pretty often, for he was held in great request by many hostesses in that city. He remained as shy of general talk as he had been when first I met him. He had *not* inherited his mother's forthgivingness. He asserted himself only when he was turned to and asked for his opinion. This he would offer with great concision. He never enlarged on it. Dr. Jowett was a little before my time, but the quality of his sayings, the rarity and the brevity of them, their startlingness, and the small high voice in which they were piped, were of course familiar to me by hearsay; and Lytton Strachey's reminded me of them. Let me quote one instance. A new book by another, a rather younger but more precocious, writer of great brilliance, my friend Philip Guedalla, had just been published. Mr. Philip Morrell said he had just been reading it, and, turning to Lytton Strachey, said, "He seems to be a sort of disciple of *yours*, Lytton." "Oh," piped Lytton, "I thought I was a disciple of his? He began before me." I say "piped" for that was what, in my hearing, he always did. And I was much interested by the statement of Mr. Leonard Woolf, who of course knew him very well and for a very long time, that in intimate conversation he would speak in a deep strong voice. I should like to have had the surprise of hearing that. I should like to have known well a man whose work has given me such deep and abiding pleasure. Some of you whom I am addressing in the University that nurtured him may have known him very well indeed, and I wish *you* were telling *me* about him instead of politely listening to my vague personal impression of him. Perhaps you will take me aside and do so when this lecture is over? But I fear you will be too tired. I shall have to await the publication of his Life and Letters.

In his lifetime his work was cordially acclaimed. He was fortunate, I think, in that the Great War (as we impresciently called it) had been going on for two and a half years before the publication of *Eminent Victorians.* In war, inevitably, rightly, voices are loud; and war, even when all the omens are propitious to our own cause, is a tragic, a painfully astringent theme. And thus the sound of a quiet voice suddenly discoursing on well-remembered figures that had flourished in halcyon years not long gone by was bound to give us something very like the sense of relief that is ours in escaping from the din and crush of a metropolis to some dear little old familiar countryside. Strachey's publishers too were fortunate in that his book was promptly praised in the course of a lecture on biography by a man of high standing. English readers are ever instantly impressionable by Prime Ministers. Mr. Gladstone had made the fortune of *Robert Elsmere.* Quite recently Lord Baldwin did like service to the work of Mary Webb. In the meantime Mr. Asquith had set the name of Lytton Strachey on the lips of all men. And Strachey's future books were by way of being what I believe is technically called "best sellers." But, as you know, great ac-

claim brings great reaction. Anatole France (with whose
spirit Strachey had so much in common) was unassailably
the Grand Old Man of French literature, and his funeral,
with all the statesmen and other dignitaries of Paris and
of the provinces following the bier along the crowd-
lined roads to Père Lachaise, was a great and moving occasion, almost on the very morrow of which Paris began
to ring with denunciations and contempt of the departed.
We are not so quick as the Latin races, and are milder.
We did not revile Tennyson or Swinburne, Meredith or
Henry James, directly after burial. But we did have fairly
prompt and fairly strong doubts about them, and were
somewhat embarrassed by the great impression they had
made on us; and if we did not succeed in forgetting them
we spoke coldly of them. Of all great modern writers
Thomas Hardy is, I think, the only one to whom death has
not brought disparagement in the interval that elapses before the justice of Time shows men in their true propor-
tions. Well, Lytton Strachey was not a great writer, not a
great man, and not old enough to have became a Grand
Old Man. But his gifts and his repute amply sufficed to
ensure reaction against him very soon after the breath was
out of his body. I think it was Ben Jonson who spoke of
"the backward kick of the dull ass's hoof." That is not a
pretty expression. But it is neither silly nor vulgar. The
vulgar term, "a debunker," the term that the average
writer or talker cursorily applies to Strachey, is not only
vulgar, it is also silly.

That he was not a hero-worshipper, or even a very gal-
lant heroine-worshipper, may be readily conceded. Also,
he was perhaps not a very warm-hearted man. (As to that,
I really don't know.) Assuredly he was not an artificer

and purveyor of plaster saints or angels. He was intensely concerned with the ramifications of human character, and greatly amused by them. He had a very independent mind, and was an egoist in so far as he liked finding things out for himself and using his own judgment on what he found. Perfect justice is a divine attribute. Lytton Strachey, being a human being, had it not. He had, like the rest of us, imperfect sympathies. Great strength of character, keen practical sense and efficiency, for example, did not cause his heart to glow so much as one might wish they had. They seemed rather to give him a slight chill. Though he recognised the greatness of Florence Nightingale, the necessary grit that was at the core of it rather jarred on him; while its absence from the character of Sidney Herbert gave great tenderness to his portrait of that statesman. Nor did his love of exercising his own judgment move him to dissent from that of Purcell, the biographer of Cardinal Manning. He was essentially, congenitally, a Newman man. Who among us isn't? But I think his preference rather blinded him to the fair amount of grit that was latent in the delicacy, the poetry of that great priest and greater writer. In the character of Dr. Arnold there was such a wealth of grit, and a strenuousness so terrific, that one may rather wonder how Strachey could bear to think of him and write of him. The portrait fails, I think, because it is composed throughout in a vein of sheer mockery. It is the only work of his that does not seek, does not hesitate, does not penetrate, and is definitely unfair. It is the only work of his that might, so far as it goes, justify the application to him of that term which shall not again soil my lips and afflict your ears.

The vein of mockery was very strong in him certainly,

and constantly asserted itself in his writings. A satirist he
was not. Mockery is a light and lambent, rather irrespon-
sible thing. *"On se moque de ce qu'on aime"* is a true saying. Strachey was always ready to mock what he loved. In
mockery there is no malice. In satire there may be plenty
of it. Pope was full of it. But he was rather an exception.
Your satirist is mostly a robust fellow, as was Aristophanes, as were Juvenal and Swift; a fellow laying about him
lustily, for the purpose of hurting, of injuring people who,
in his opinion, ought to be hurt and injured. He may, like
Aristophanes, have an abundant, a glorious gift for mockery. But fundamentally he is grim. He is grimly concerned
with what he hates in the age to which he belongs. I do
not remember having found anywhere in the works of
Lytton Strachey one passing reference to any current
event. He was quite definitely, and quite impenitently,
what in current jargon is called an escapist.

Need we be angry? It takes all kinds to make a world,
or even to make a national literature. Even for spirits less
fastidious than Strachey's, there is, even at the best of
times, a great charm in the past. Time, that sedulous artist,
has been at work on it, selecting and rejecting with great
tact. The past is a work of art, free from irrelevancies and
loose ends. There are, for our vision, comparatively few
people in it, and all of them are interesting people. The
dullards have all disappeared—all but those whose dull-
ness was so pronounced as to be in itself for us an amusing virtue. And in the past there is so blessedly nothing for
us to worry about. Everything is settled. There's nothing
to be done about it—nothing but to contemplate it and
blandly form theories about this or that aspect of it.
Strachey was by temperament an eighteenth-century man.

In the Age of Reason, and of Wit too, he felt far more at home than in the aftermath of the Industrial Revolution, and in the first fine careless rapture of the Internal Combustion Engine. Even we, in spite of our coarseness, deplore these great phenomena, and wish they had never happened, and grieve that mankind will not in any foreseeable future be able to shake them off and be quit of them. Strachey, like the good eighteenth-century Englishman that he was, had close contacts with France. Indeed I feel that he was even more at ease in French than in English literature and life. It was in that handbook on French literature that he made his debut. In the volume entitled *Books and Characters* (published in 1922) and in his last work, *Portraits in Miniature* (1931), there is constant truancy to France. Racine, Voltaire, Rousseau, Mme de Sévigné, the Abbé Morellet, Mme du Deffand, the Président de Brosses—with all of these he is on terms of cosiest intimacy. To our native Victorians he was rather in the relation of a visitor, an inquirer, an inquisitor. I don't think he was—as Desmond MacCarthy had gathered from him that he was—"horrified" by them. He disliked the nineteenth century in comparison with its forerunner, but it appealed to him far more than could the twentieth. Machinery, science and applied science, had not yet got a really firm grip on England, and moreover, in spite of one Reform Bill after another, government was still oligarchic. Inequality flourished almost as much as ever. Barriers were almost as ever high. The seeds of standardisation and of mass production had not been even sown. Life was full of salient variety, of idiosyncrasy, of oddity, of character, character untrammelled. Giles Lytton Strachey (I feel that I ought to have said this at the outset) was born on March the first, 1880. And therefore when, in his maturity, he began to write about the Victorians he was old enough to know his way about and among them, having been nurtured among elders to whom they were familiar; and he was young enough to feel far away from them, to be curious about them, to be wondering at them greatly. The immediate past, the time that one almost belongs to—almost but not quite—is peculiarly tantalising. Perhaps Strachey was rather ashamed of the hold the Victorians had on him in virtue of their proximity. And perhaps it was for this reason, and to shake off these insidious rivals to his dear ones of the eighteenth century, or perhaps it was merely in a sudden spirit of adventure, that he plunged off into the court of Queen Elizabeth. Anyway it was a brave thing to do. *Elizabeth and Essex* (published in 1928) is a finely constructed work, but seems to me to be essentially guesswork. A very robustious, slapdash writer might convince me that he was in close touch with the souls of those beings whose actions and motives are to me as mysterious as those of wild animals in an impenetrable jungle. You rightly infer that I am *not* a sixteenth-century man. And I make so bold as to say "Neither was Lytton Strachey."

"A finely constructed work" I have said. But what work of Lytton Strachey's, large or small, was not admirably firm in structure?—*totus, teres atque rotundus.* I make no apology for that tag: it is so often forgotten by gifted authors. Let us not ignore the virtue of form in literature. It is the goblet for the wine. Be the wine never so good, is not our enjoyment of it diminished if the hospitable vintner pours it forth to be lapped up by us from the ground with our tongues? Improvisation is the essence of good talk. Heaven defend us from the talker who doles out things prepared for us! But let heaven not less defend us from the beautifully spontaneous writer who puts his trust in the inspiration of the moment!—unless indeed he be a man of genius, of genius that creates for him a rough but sufficing form in his wild career. No writer need despise literary form as something artificial and unworthy of him. Nature herself, with her flowers and her trees, with many of her hills and streams and valleys, even with some of her human beings, is an ardent and unashamed formalist. I would advise any young writer—or any middle-aged or old one who may be needing advice—to think out carefully, before he begins his novel, or biography, or essay, or what-not, the shape that it should have. I would say to him—quoting another excellent Horatian tag—*Respice finem*. Let him before he begins know just how he is going to end. And I would, at the risk of boring him, insist that the beginning is not less important than the end, and that what comes between them is no less important than they. In journalism, I have often been told, the first sentence is the thing that matters most. Grip the reader's attention, and all will be well. I am not sure that this is so. Not long before the outbreak of war, when paper was very plentiful, I saw in an evening paper a signed article about Karl Marx. The first sentence was as follows: "Deep down in a grave at the Highgate the corpse of Karl Marx lies rotting." So far, so good. But what followed was a quite mild and well-reasoned depreciation of that writer's doctrines. The average reader, the man in the street, had been gripped only to be disappointed. Well, literature is not read in the street. Streets are not what they were when Thomas Macaulay would walk from the Albany to Clapham Common reading Sophocles all the way. Literature is read in homes only, and I fancy that in those quiet surroundings the reader of it should at the outset be rather invited, engaged, allured, than gripped. Indeed, I think you will find that in all periods good poets or writers of prose have, whether in long or in short works, made quiet beginnings. Quiet endings, too. The reader, they have all instinctively felt, should be lifted gently out of himself, and borne up and up, and along, and in due course be set down gently, to remember his adventure.

Strachey, certainly, had this good instinct, and obeyed it always. James Boswell, describing the conversation of members of The Club, recorded the delight of watching Edmund Burke "winding himself like a serpent into his subject." Even so was Strachey wont to wind himself into his subject—and eventually out of it—suavely. Let me quote, as an instance, the opening and the closing words of the essay on the Abbé Morellet (a disciple of Diderot, a favoured friend of Mme Helvétius, and at one time a quite well-treated prisoner in the Bastille):

> Talleyrand once remarked that only those who had lived in France before the Revolution had really experienced *la douceur de vivre*. The Abbé Morellet would have agreed with him. Born in 1727 at Lyons, the son of a small paper merchant, how was it possible, in that age of caste and privilege, that André Morellet should have known anything of life but what was hard, dull, and insignificant?

Then comes the tale of the Abbé's career, beautifully told, and concluding with this picture of his old age, when he used to sit dozing by the fire in the drawing-room of young Mme de Rémusat:

He was treated with great respect by everybody; even the First Consul was flattering; even the Emperor was polite, and made him a Senator. Then the Emperor disappeared, and a Bourbon ruled on the throne of his fathers. With that tenacity of life which seems to have been the portion of the creatures of the eighteenth century, Morellet continued in this world until his ninety-second year. But this world was no longer what it used to be: something had gone wrong. Those agitations, those arrangements and rearrangements, they seemed hardly worth attending to. One might as well doze. All his young friends were very kind certainly, but did they understand? How could they? What had been their experience of life? As for him, ah! *he* had listened to Diderot —used to sit for hours talking in the Tuileries Gardens with D'Alembert and Mademoiselle de Lespinasse— mentioned by Voltaire—spent half a life-time at Auteuil with dear Madame Helvétius—imprisoned in the Bastille . . . he nodded. Yes! *He* had known *la douceur de vivre.*

Exquisitely beautiful, that diminuendo, is it not? And as tender as it is profound. I have said that Strachey was not, for aught I knew, a warm-hearted man. A tender-hearted man he assuredly was.

As biographer, he had, besides his gift for construction, the advantage of a splendid gift for narrative. He was a masterly teller of tales, long or short, tragic or comic. He could, as it were, *see* the thing he had to tell, *see* the people concerned in it, see them outwardly and inwardly, and make us share gratefully his vision. Who could have made so much as he of such things as the adventures of "the boy Jones' in Buckingham Palace, of the inception and the building of the Albert Memorial, of Mr. Gorham's vicissitudes in the Court of Arches and the Judicial Committee of the Privy Council? As the finest example of his narrative gift—I had almost said his dramatic gift—I would choose perhaps his treatment of what led up to the tragedy of the dereliction and death of General Gordon. The tremendous tale, charged with the strangely diverse characters of the eminent men involved in it—Gladstone, Hartington, Baring, and Gordon himself—is told with the subtlest strength, oscillating steadily, with the swing of a pendulum, between Downing Street and the Soudan. For a while we are in one place, then we are with equal vividness in the other, alternately, repeatedly; and great is the cumulative effect of this prolonged strophe and antistrophe. To those of you who are, as I am, fond of thrills, but have never read these pages, I would say earnestly, "Read these pages."

The element of criticism was implicit, and often explicit, in all Lytton Strachey's biographical work. From time to time he indulged in criticism undiluted. As a literary critic alone he would have been worthy to be remembered. The best kind of critic—the helpfully interpretative, the almost creative critic—is very passive before he becomes active. Such an one was Strachey. With an intellect of steely quality there was combined in him a deep sensibility and receptivity. He had felt before he thought. And two at least of his critical works—his long essay on Racine, and his Leslie Stephen Lecture on Pope—happened to be of cardinal, of crucial effect. Racine had never had high repute upon these shores; and the Romantic Movement had reduced Pope to a small shadow among our own poets. It was Strachey's silver trumpet that woke the young men of two decades ago to high ap-

preciation of those two worthies. And by the way, literature apart, aren't there in the Elysian Fields two other
worthies who have reason to be grateful to the supposed
iconoclast?—Queen Victoria and the Prince Consort?
The Prince in his life-time had never been popular; and
after Sir Theodore Martin's saccharine biography he had
become a veritable mock. I never heard a kind word for
him. The Queen, who in my childhood and youth had
been not only revered but worshipped, was, soon after her
death, no longer in public favour. Her faults had become
known, and her virtues were unheeded. This is not so
now; and is not so by reason of Lytton Strachey's fully
judicial presentment of her with all the faults over which
her virtues so very much preponderated. And it is, by the
same token, through him that we know the Prince not as
just dreadfully admirable, but as someone to be loved and
to be sorry for.

But after all—and perhaps you are saying "Oh, if only
it *were* all!"—it is as a writer, in the strict sense, as a user
of that very beautiful medium, the English language, that
I would especially extol Lytton Strachey. There is such a
word as *prosaist*. It is a word that we never use; whereas
prosateur is not seldom on the lips of Frenchmen, and is
spoken in a very serious tone, a tone as serious as that in
which we use the word *poet*. Frenchmen are keenly aware
of the virtues of prose, and we, not being so, have accepted the idea that French prose is superior to ours. Undoubtedly, the general level of it is so. The average
Frenchman writes better prose than the average Englishman. His medium is a language whose greatly prevailing
Latinity makes it far more lucid than ours. It is, more-

over, a language that has been by authority kept free from corruption. We have had no Richelieu, and if we had we would not, in our sturdy independence, have bowed down to the mandarins of his creation. Our prosaists, to achieve lucidity and euphony, have to do a good deal of filtration on the way. I remember Lytton Strachey once said to me, in reference to this need, that he wished he were a Frenchman, writing in French. I rather shocked him by saying "Oh, any fool can write good French prose." But truth is in itself so good a thing that one may be pardoned for exaggerating it every now and then. Good English is, I am sure, far less easy to write than good French; and *"pour être difficile la tâche n'est que plus glorieuse";* and difficulties surmounted (though only had they not been surmounted would the reader be conscious of them) do somehow, I am convinced, enrich the texture of good writing. The English language, being part Latin, part Saxon, is, in my rough insular opinion, an even finer medium than the French one. Latin is, one might say, its bony structure, Saxon its flesh and blood. And of these two Latin is perhaps the more important. A skeleton by itself is a noble thing, whereas an inchoate mass of flesh and blood is not. A writer who has not in boyhood been well grounded in Latin is at a grievous disadvantage. However keen a natural instinct he may have for writing, he will be diffuse, he will be sloppy, as was, for example, D. H. Lawrence, whose prose was so dangerous a model for young admirers of his philosophy. The Latin element, on the other hand, should not have too strong a hold on a writer, leading him to over-great austerity and nobility, even to aridity, as happened so often in the seventeenth and eighteenth centuries. In the best writing neither element prevails. The two merge indistinguishably in each other.

To single Lytton Strachey out as a born writer would be to offend a great number of people. For there is a very widespread and comfortable belief that we are all of us born writers. Not long ago I heard that agile and mellifluous quodlibetarian, Dr. Joad, saying in answer to a questioner who wanted to write good letters, that anybody could write good letters: one had but to think out clearly what one wanted to say, and then set it down in the simplest terms. And a few weeks later, when the writing of books was under discussion, he said that the writers who thought most about how they should write were the hardest to read; and again he seemed to think lucidity all-sufficing. I admit that Herbert Spencer had also, many years ago, seemed to think so, and said so. But I maintain that had he not thought so, had Nature at the outset endowed him fully with a gift for writing, we should all of us be now reading him with greater zest and constancy than we do. A true gift for writing, though in spite of the telephone we all do still write letters sometimes, and though authors of books are more than ever numerous, is not widely bestowed. Nor is a true gift for painting, or for playing the violin; and of that we are somehow aware. We do not say to a violinist "Just think out clearly what you want to express and then go straight ahead. Never mind how you handle your bow," nor to a painter, "Got your subject and your scheme of colour in your head all right, eh? Then don't bother about how you lay your paints on, dear old boy." Let us not make similar remarks to writers. I am willing to concede that in the eighteen-nineties perhaps rather too much thought was given to *manner* in literature. The young men of that decade were perhaps over-influenced by the example of such elders as Walter Pater and Robert Louis Stevenson, overfond of unusual words and peculiar cadences. Preciosity is a fault on the right side; but it is a fault. A venial one? Yes, in Pater, the essayist. But not in Stevenson, the novelist, when he was telling a straightforward story and wishing to give the reader an illusion of reality. From such books as *Treasure Island* and *The Master of Ballantrae* I have never for one moment had that illusion, have been too acutely and delightedly conscious of the technical graces and ingenuities of the author. When Stevenson did not aim at realism, and was entirely oblivious of Sir Walter Scott, and was giving rein to his own riotous sense of fantasy, as in *The New Arabian Nights,* or *The Dynamiter*, or *The Wrong Box*, the jewelled elaboration of the manner becomes an integral part of the fun, and keeps us laughing the more irresistibly and the more loudly. These books are, I think, far and away his best—the most characteristic of himself, of his true and magical self. I have always regretted that Maurice Hewlett, one of the lights of the 'nineties and of later years, was not a humourist and wished to illude us with his tales; for his preciosity was fatal to his wish. Besides, it was a robust preciosity; and that is unnatural, is a contradiction in terms.

I conceive that had Lytton Strachey been a young man in those 'nineties, and not the merely growing boy that he was in most of them, he might have inclined to preciosity. Of this you will find no jot in his prose. His manner, though classical, is entirely natural, and rather shy. He makes no attempt to dazzle. He is not even afraid of cli-

chés. He can be very homely. When he is narrating something humdrum he is quite congruously pedestrian;
though even then felicities are apt to come shining forth
by the way; as, for instance, in his account of how the
young Queen Victoria's popularity was restored by the
happiness of her marriage.

> The middle classes, in particular, were pleased. They
> liked a love-match; they liked a household in which they
> seemed to see reflected, as in some resplendent looking-
> glass, the ideal image of the very lives they lived them-
> selves. Their own existences, less exalted, but oh! so
> soothingly similar, acquired an added excellence, an
> added succulence, from the early hours, the regularity,
> the plain tuckers, the round games, the roast beef and
> Yorkshire pudding of Osborne.

His manner is infinitely flexible, in accord to every varia-
tion of whatever his theme may be. Consider the differences between his ways of writing about Lord Melbourne,
Lord Palmerston, Mr. Disraeli, and Mr. Gladstone. His
manner seems to bring us into the very presence of these
widely disparate Premiers. Note the mellow and leisurely
benignity of the cadences in which he writes of Lord Melbourne—"the autumn rose," as he called him. Note the
sharp brisk straightforward buoyancy of the writing whenever Lord Palmerston appears; and the elaborate Oriental
richness of manner when Mr. Disraeli is on the scene.
And does not all the subtlety of M. Gladstone confront us
when we are asked, "What, then, was the truth? In the
physical universe there are no chimeras. But man is more
various than nature; was Mr. Gladstone perhaps a chi-
mera of the spirit? Did his very essence lie in the confu-
sion of incompatibles? His very essence? It eludes the

hand that grasps it. One is baffled, as his political opponents were fifty years ago. The soft serpent coils harden into quick strength that has vanished, leaving only emptiness and perplexity behind." I can't help repeating to you the first words of that last sentence. "The soft serpent coils harden into quick strength that has vanished." Was ever speed so well suggested as in those eleven words?—words of a born writer, and a taker, we may be sure, of infinite pains.

If I were asked what seemed to me the paramount quality of Lytton Strachey's prose, I should reply, in one word, Beauty. That is perhaps a rather old-fashioned word, a word jarring to young writers, and to young painters or musicians, and by them associated with folly, with vanity and frivolity. To me it is still a noble word, and I fancy it will some day come back into fashion. I believe that the quality it connotes is essential to all the arts. The stress and strain, the uncertainty of life in the past thirty years has not, I think, been favourable to the arts, though in those years a great deal of admirable work has of course been done (mostly, alas, by men of maturish years). Nor do I suppose that in my time, or until long after my time, will very propitious conditions supervene. There is a spate of planning for the future of many things. Perhaps some people are at this moment strenuously planning for the future of the arts. But I doubt whether in the equalitarian era for which we are heading—the era in which we shall have built Jerusalem on England's smooth and asphalt land—the art of literature, which throve so finely and so continuously from Elizabethan to paulo-post-Victorian days, will have a wonderful renascence. We are told on high authority, from both sides of the Atlantic, that the present century is to be the Century of the Common Man. We are all of us to go down on our knees and clasp our hands and raise our eyes and worship the Common Man. I am not a learned theologian, but I think I am right in saying that this religion has at least the hall-mark of novelty—has never before been propagated, even in the East, from which so many religions have sprung. Well, I am an old man, and old men are not ready converts to new religions. This one does not stir my soul. I take some comfort in the fact that its propagators do not seek to bind us to it for ever. *"This,"* they say, "is to be the Century of the Common Man." I like to think that on the morning of January the first, in the year 2000, mankind will be free to unclasp its hands and rise from its knees and look about it for some other, and perhaps more national, form of faith. I like also to think that in the meantime, in the great pale platitude of the meantime, there will be, as hitherto, a few discriminating readers of things written in past times; people likely to read, and likely to revel in, the works of Lytton Strachey. After all, it is always by the devotion of a few only that good books become classics.

I dont know whether it is "in order" to dedicate a Rede Lecture to anybody. If it is, I would like to dedicate this one to the memory of Lytton Strachey. I am always very proud that he dedicated one of his books, his last one, to me. Forgive me for boasting that he said "with gratitude and admiration." To him I dedicate this lecture with far greater gratitude than ever he can have felt to me, and with far deeper admiration than ever he can have had for anything of mine.

THE CAMBRIDGE UNIVERSITY REDE LECTURE, 1943

A NOTE ON THE AUTHOR

BORN AT LONDON on August 24, 1872, Henry Maximilian Beerbohm was known to several generations as "Max" before, in 1939, he was knighted. He was, of course, a half-brother of Sir Herbert Beerbohm Tree. Known from his youth as a mordant writer and caricaturist, Beerbohm satirically published in 1896 a small book entitled *The Works of Max Beerbohm,* complete with bibliography. In that year, too, he followed George Bernard Shaw as drama critic of the *Saturday Review* (London), a post he held until 1910. Then, after his marriage to an American actress, Florence Kahn of Memphis, Tennessee, he settled at Rapallo in Italy, his home for the rest of his life. (The first Lady Beerbohm died in 1951. The second Lady Beerbohm was Elizabeth Jungmann, whom he married shortly before his death.)

The published books of the "Incomparable Max," as Shaw called him, include both prose volumes and collections of caricatures: *More, Yet Again, And Even Now, A Christmas Garland, The Happy Hypocrite, Zuleika Dobson, Seven Men, The Dreadful Dragon of Hay Hill, Caricatures of Twenty-Five Gentlemen, The Poet's Corner, A Book of Caricatures, The Second Childhood of John Bull, Fifty Caricatures, A Survey, Rossetti and His Circle, Things New and Old, Observations,* and *Around Theatres.*

Sir Max died at Rapallo on May 20, 1956.

A NOTE ON THE TYPE

The text of this book was set on the Linotype in a face called TIMES ROMAN, *designed by* STANLEY MORISON *for* The Times *(London), and first introduced by that newspaper in the middle nineteen thirties.*

Among typographers and designers of the twentieth century, Stanley Morison has been a strong forming influence, as typographical adviser to the English Monotype Corporation, as a director of two distinguished English publishing houses, and as a writer of sensibility, erudition, and keen practical sense.

In 1930 Morison wrote: "Type design moves at the pace of the most conservative reader. The good type-designer therefore realizes that, for a new fount to be successful, it has to be so good that only very few recognize its novelty. If readers do not notice the consummate reticence and rare discipline of a new type, it is probably a good letter." It is now generally recognized that in the creation of Times Roman *Morison successfully met the qualifications of this theoretical doctrine.*

Composed, printed, and bound by The Plimpton Press, Norwood, Massachusetts. Paper manufactured by P. H. Glatfelter Company, Spring Grove, Pennsylvania. Designed by

WARREN CHAPPELL